Working Man's Jesus

ROGER LEE

Working Man's Jesus

Copyright © 2013 by Roger Lee

ISBN 978-0-615-83393-4

Editing and formatting by ChristianEditingServices.com

Cover design by Sterling Printing & Graphics

Cover photos from iStockphoto.com

TABLE OF CONTENTS

Acknowledgments

It would be remiss of me not to offer a word of thanks to those who helped and inspired me as I wrote Working Man's Jesus. I thank God most of all for who He is and for what He has done in my life. While writing this book, I realized something very important: I want and need God to be my everything. No matter how the journey of this life goes, without Him, I am nothing. Without Him, I have no tomorrows.

I want to thank my wife, who allowed me the time and encouraged me to keep writing even when I didn't feel like it. To my son I say, I thank you and love you with all my heart. I know listening to Dad's writings was not at the top of your "wow list" of things to do. But being who you are, you smiled, offered words of wisdom, and loved me all the same.

Pastor Tony Rea, without you, I could have never written this book. No, it wasn't only your inspired thoughts or instruction about writing but rather your heart full of God's grace. Your example has changed my life forever. Your ministry as senior pastor at Community Christian Church has touched so many lives.

To Senior Pastor Douglas Schmidt at Woodside Bible Church, thank you for having a vision to reach the world at any cost. Thank you for your support and friendship and thank you most of all for your godly walk that I have had the privilege of observing time and time again. You lifted me up even in moments when Satan was doing his best to pull me down.

I also must thank my dear lifelong friend Pastor Rodney Friend. Rodney is my hero. He laid down everything he has for the cause of reaching the lost. His life has been full of fleshly disappointments and trials. Yet he never turned away from his

Lord and Savior, Jesus Christ. Rodney, you may not know it, but in this life, you will always be my champion. Because of you, my dear brother, I was able to finish this book.

And what can I say about my brother in Christ Pastor Stacey Johnson? He is a small town pastor with a heart that could cover the world. Pastor of toilet repair one day, then preaching at a funeral the next, or leading some soul to Jesus. Stacey, you may never pastor a large church and they may never put your name up in lights, but your friendship and brotherly love have held me up in the darkest moments. You are one of the reasons I will see Jesus and my dear Candace.

For sure I must thank the team of people who helped me page after page. Without your skills and support, this book would never have come to completion. And a special thanks to Roger Simmons and Stephanie Nickel. You may never know just how much God has used you and the impact your lives will make on others who read these pages.

Last but not the least, I thank my brother in Christ and forever friend Pete Pappas. Your daily phone calls, our hunts together, talks about life's ups and downs, laughter and tears have helped me on this journey we call life. No words can ever express my thanks or love for you. God knew just who and what I needed when He sent you my way.

Thank you, God, for all these people as well as the many others who impact me day after day—even when they don't know it. You have given me a great team. I thank all of you and most of all, I thank God for allowing me the honor of reaching out to other men with this book.

Chapter 1

Woe Is Me!

EVER HAD A SEASON IN YOUR LIFE WHEN EVERYTHING WAS JUST plain miserable? Maybe you're in one now.

The boss tells you they're downsizing and he'll have to let you go. You get home and find out your son has been suspended from school. Your test results are back and the doctor says he has bad news.

So who am I to address your problems? You already know me—even if we haven't met face to face—because you know yourself.

I've experienced hard times. Financial setbacks. Relationship challenges. Spiritual uncertainty. And during the darkest of nights, my daughter Candace, who had faced life-threatening health issues from birth, passed away while we were on a vacation cruise.

My story is nothing new—and neither is yours. Men like you and me have been facing issues like these for thousands of years. Do you know about Job from the Old Testament? He was living the good life. He was a very successful family man. And one day he was the subject of a discussion between God and Satan. I imagine their conversation might have gone something like this.

"Hey, God, you're pretty proud of your man Job, aren't you?"

"Very proud," God said. "So proud . . . I'll tell you what, Satan. I'll lower my fortress walls of blessing and protection and let you toy with his life a little. You can make his life utterly miserable, but you can't touch him."

Satan agreed to the terms. All kinds of bombs and ballistic missiles began dropping on Job. Talk about stealth targeting! The devil hit him with everything but a nuclear blast. First, Job learned all his camels, sheep, donkeys, and oxen—more than 10,000 animals—had been stolen or killed. Not long afterward, he learned his workers had been taken as slaves or murdered. And if this wasn't already enough bad news, our man Job learned his children and their families had been killed when a fierce wind leveled the house they were in.

Unbelievably, Satan went before the Lord again and asked if he could have yet another go at poor Job. God agreed. Satan visited Job once again and left him covered with painful, itchy boils.

By this time, Job had no one—no servants or family, except for his wife. His wealth had evaporated and he was left in excruciating physical pain. He had gone from the highest of highs to the lowest of lows. Ever been there?

Job cried out, "I wish I had never been born. Why didn't you simply leave me as dirt in the earth, God? I have no peace, no quietness. I have no rest, only turmoil."

Have you ever regretted the day *you* were born?

That awful day aboard ship in May 2009, I had a pretty good idea of how Job must have felt.

11

So much happened to poor Job in a short time. Our miserable friend wanted nothing more than to end it all. Wouldn't you know it? Along came Mrs. Job but not with the encouragement you might expect or hope for.

For better or worse, huh?

What wisdom did Job's dearly beloved give him? "Job honey, I've thought long and hard on the matter and I've concluded your life is hopeless. So, after much consideration and looking at your life insurance policy . . ." (sorry, my humor; it's not in the Bible) ". . . why don't you curse God and die?"

Her words must have stunned our man. I can imagine Job's face said it all. I can almost hear his reply. "So, let me get this straight, oh dear and caring wife. As long as things are going well, you want us to call on the great God of the heavens. Do I have that right? But now that we've lost everything, the best advice you can offer me is to swear at God, have a massive heart attack, and keel over dead?"

"Well," a thoughtful Mrs. Job replied, "since you put it that way . . . I suppose so."

To make matters worse, along came Job's friends. They may have been well intentioned, but they missed the mark . . . by several hundred miles.

Eliphaz, Bildad, and Zophar came to save the day for good ol' Job. Each of them had an opinion about why Job was in such a terrible state. They had lots to say, so I'll jump ahead. Instead of encouraging and comforting him, their "insights" caused him to question God and His nature even more. Job's mind was clouded and his heart crushed. He couldn't figure out if all the calamities happened because of something he had done or something somebody in his family had done—or if God was simply mad at him.

Ever been there? Ever cried out, "Why God? Why is this happening to me?"

Have you ever been in a place where life was purring along one day and pure hell the next? Sure you have. We all have at one time or another. And where does our help come from? Not even family or friends can help all the time, but God can.

Job's so-called comforters stirred up several thoughts about his life and about God. In fact, he began questioning the Lord's motives and purpose. Job even thought about asking, "Do you really know what you're doing up there?"

Eliphaz, Bildad, and Zophar had exhausted Job with all their Fortune 500 opinions. His ears were pounding and his head was rattled. He couldn't take any more of their "wisdom." Now I wasn't there, but if I had been, I would have offered Job a set of earplugs and two aspirins.

In Job 16, Job "thanked" the three for all their words of misery. Up to his ears with their advice, Job had had enough. His radiator was steaming as he began to reply to his so-called tactical support group.

"You guys are miserable comforters. You all stink if you're trying to help me. You're long-winded and you argue. Surely, O God, you have worn me out" (Job 16:7).

In this Old Testament story, there was still one more man to hear from. But first, let's recap.

Job had lost everything. His friends brought him their opinions and suggestions, which did nothing but create more frustration. Even his wife suggested he curse God and die.

Although his buddies didn't come to the right conclusions about why Job was facing such overwhelming pain and heartache, Job did have his moments of pride. In chapter thirty, one might think he was speaking with a little too much self-centeredness. Earlier in the story, he expressed his concern about men mocking him. In fact, he said they spat on him, kept their distance, and detested him. He talked about losing his dignity and about how God threw him in the mud. Job was focusing on himself and his woes. Sound familiar?

When we fail and our pride is beaten down, many times we blame others for our mistakes and failures. Verse after verse of chapter thirty illustrates Job whining before God as if to say, "I'm a great guy, so why have you done all these bad things to me?"

He said he had cried out to God, but God hadn't listened as He had previously. Job said God threw him into storms. He accused the Lord of being ruthless and even said the Almighty had attacked him.

"Poor, poor me! Life couldn't have been better. God, you gave me everything a man could ask for—even more. I was well respected by everyone. I had wealth beyond measure. My family and my sons and their wives were well taken care of. No matter where I traveled, people looked up to me. And now, for reasons I can't explain, you've destroyed my life. You've taken my wealth, my family, and my health. You've made them vanish before me. I've taken care of my workers, treated my wife and kids great, helped my neighbors, and given to those in need. So why in the world have you destroyed my life? Why, oh Lord, have you made a mess of me?"

Sound familiar? Are you a person who has done right by everyone—at least most of the time? Have you worked hard all your life, helped your friends and family, and given to the poor? For all your good conduct and intentions, the results are anything but fruitful in your eyes. Been there.

Everyone around us knows we're nice guys and keep mostly to ourselves. But the big question is this: Is this what the Almighty wants for our life? Are we pursuing our own adventure or His? Yes, we can justify our life and argue our case all we want, but He is still God and always will be. Don't ever think otherwise. And sometimes He sends someone along with insight far beyond anything we expect.

He or she, a true champion, will take the bull by the horns. These true friends—or heroes as I like to call them—come to us with words of truth, hope, and God-inspired instruction. Elihu was just such a hero in Job's life.

Elihu was a young man who accompanied Job's three well-meaning friends. So far in the story, he had not been allowed to speak. I can imagine while traveling to meet with Job, Bildad, Zophar, and Eliphaz said something along these lines: "Elihu, we're going to see our friend Job. He's in a bad way and we're on our way to cheer him up. Now you can come along if you'd like, but you're young and not as smart as we are, so keep quiet. Just watch and learn from us. Understand?"

But by the time the three finished carving up Job, Elihu had heard about all his ears and stomach could handle. Enough was enough. So he said, "Excuse me, guys, but this is a crock. And, Job, I have to tell you that all your self-righteous talk is making me ill. Do you really believe what you're saying? Are you really going to soak in all this garbage these three are feeding you? Really!

"I'm young, so I've kept my mouth shut out of respect. I had hoped Bildad and the others would give you sound wisdom and instruction, but hey, are you kidding me?

"My words," Elihu continued, "come with no selfish motivation. Mine are from the Spirit of God, who speaks through me. You say, Job, you are without sin and have no faults, yet God has found fault in you. You're going back and forth like a boat being tossed on the sea. You've told your self-righteous story to anyone who would listen—and even to God. Now let me tell you who God is, what His hands have made, and how great is the One you seem to have forgotten and want to pick a fight with."

Dramatic? Maybe. Truthful? For sure. Elihu laid it on the line for our dear brother Job. He said, "Hey, Job, if you sin, do you think it affects God? Or if you are righteous, what does it offer Him? God does not answer men who are arrogant. He doesn't listen to your empty pleas, Job."

Although Elihu's words are hard to swallow, if you look in chapter thirty-six, you'll see he also offers Job words of hope. "God delivers the afflicted," Elihu said, "and He watches over the righteous. God does not despise you, Job, even though you've let your mouth get you into trouble."

Like the others, Elihu had a lot to say, but let's move on to Job's one-on-one with God Almighty.

As we know, Job found his life going from one mess to another. Although he couldn't see it, God had been allowing these things to happen for His glory—and ultimately, for Job's good. But instead of remaining silent, our man Job decided to pick a fight with the Great I Am.

I can see it now. "Ladies and gentlemen, in this corner, standing six feet tall, weighing 210 pounds is Job from the land of Uz. His corner men are Eliphaz, Bildad, and Zophar.

"And in this corner, standing taller than the highest mountain and weighing more than all the planets and stars in the universe is God, the Eternal One, the Alpha and Omega, the Lord of lords, Maker of heaven and earth. In His corner are all the angels in heaven."

The proverbial bell rang and the verbal fight began. Job was silly enough to lead by questioning God's actions and implied the Lord was not who He said He was. "If you are

God Almighty, why have you forgotten your servant Job? Why have you let me down, God?"

Not your most shining moment, Job.

And then God speaks. "I am about to open my mouth" (Job 33:2).

Whoa! I think if the Maker of heaven and earth informs us He has something to say, it's best to close our mouth and listen.

God had had His fill of Job's pity party. "Enough is enough. Keep quiet and listen to what I, the Lord God, have to say to you. Job, did you make the earth? Did you make the stars? What about the wind? Is it your doing?"

After speaking at length, God paused to let Job get in a few words. Job came to his senses. "God, I forgot just who you are and what you have done. Yes, Lord, I've listened to some bad advice. I went on a self-righteous, woe is me trip. Forgive me, God, for not trusting you in all things. Please do with me as you please. I know you have my best interests at heart."

Job's story ends with God restoring all he had lost and more. He was blessed with a long life and a family who supported and encouraged him.

And although I still face challenges, God has abundantly blessed me as well. My business is thriving. I have the health and strength to work long hours. I have ministry opportunities within my church and beyond. I am richly blessed with a wife and son—although we will miss our precious Candace until we are reunited with her in heaven.

God is still God and that's just the way it is.

Consider the summary and questions below and look to the God of the universe for truth and guidance for your journey through life.

In Summary

I've condensed the forty-two chapters of Job into just a few pages. Perhaps you can see yourself in Job's story. I pray you've picked up a few pointers for your relationship with God. I encourage you to remember this:

- Tragedy comes to everyone at one time or another, even to the righteous.

- Your family may mean well, but always keep your eyes on God.

- Know that Satan will do everything he can to keep you separated from God's best for your life.

- Fear, doubt, and hopelessness are but some of the ways Satan sets out to destroy your life. These things are not from God.

- Don't blame God.

- Study God's Word and look for wise council from godly men. Keep your ears closed to the world's opinions.

- Always remember that pride kills. Live humbly before God and see how He blesses your life.

- Don't let material things dictate your eternity. You won't like the results.

- When the storms of life come, seek God first, foremost, and continually. Make prayer your first choice—not your last resort.

- When things are going well, give the Lord praise. When things are going badly, give the Lord praise.

- Once you've had your say with God, it's always better to zip up and listen because He *will* speak.

- Know that God wants the very best for you even when He uses the rod of correction.

- Finally, God cares for you and loves you even when you fail. He wants to have a growing relationship with you.

When we let His will become ours, the Lord Jesus offers hope. It's so great that our loving heavenly Father forgives us when we confess our sins, our failings. Whether it's with a spouse, the in-laws, one of our children, a co-worker, or a one-time friend, we can make a change for the better in our relationships. Try living your life God's way. It works.

Fall to your knees, and tell God the truth: "Lord, I need you."

Talk to Him. Yes, really talk to Him. You don't have to use high and mighty words. You don't have to use some special tone of voice. Simply lay it on the line. "God, I need you every day of my life."

Be direct. Talk about your marriage. Ask Him for guidance in raising your children. Speak boldly with Him about your job and your financial needs. Pour out your heart with everything you have.

And know this: He is a jealous God. This means you are to give Him—and only Him—your praise. Let the God who holds your life in His hands hear you acknowledge Him as the King of kings and Lord of lords.

The next step may be extremely hard for some of us, but

it must be done. Be quiet and listen. We must let our ears, heart, and soul be attentive. The God of the universe will speak in His time and in His way if we let Him. Just ask Job.

I'll bet you and I have many things in common with our man Job. I know the Lord did. In Luke 22:42, Jesus pleads, "Father, if you are willing, take this cup from me; yet not my will, but yours be done." In His humanity, He did not want to face the physical, emotional, and spiritual pain of crucifixion. Even so, He submitted to His Father's will.

If you're having troubles and feel like giving up on life and on God, I offer these words to you: Hold on. Victory in Jesus is on its way. The battles you face may not be won today, tomorrow, or even the next day, but if you trust in the Lord Jesus Christ, a new day is coming.

Consider this . . .

1. Describe a time when you felt everything was going against you. How did you respond? What did you learn?

2. Describe a time when well-meaning friends only made you feel worse. How did you respond? Would you respond differently if you had it to do over again? If so, how?

3. Are you sometimes reluctant to accept responsibility for your mistakes? Do you blame others? Why? What steps are you willing to take to begin taking responsibility when you do wrong?

4. In what areas of your life are you pursuing your own agenda instead of God's? Name one step you are willing to take this week to move into line with His plan for your life.

Chapter 2
Bull Riding Storms

THE RULES ARE SIMPLE. PLACE A 150-POUND COWBOY ON THE back of a snorting, ground-shaking, two-thousand-pound bull. Have him hold onto a piece of rope with one hand and see if he can stay on the animal's back for eight eternal seconds. Sounds like something we all should try.

Equipment includes one piece of flat, braided rope. The rider should also have a pair of cowboy boots, rosin for grip, leather gloves, and chaps. That's all he needs—that and ample amounts of courage or foolhardiness, depending on your perspective.

Judges score the ride from 0 to 100. Besides the eight-second requirement, judges base the ride on the bull's strength, health, agility, and age. The tougher and meaner the bull, the more exciting the ride is expected to be. By the way, the motivation to get a perfect score runs high. No one on the pro circuit has ever done it.

Excitement scores big in bull riding. People love a thrill—when someone *else* is facing danger. The cowboy who faces that danger successfully and rides the meanest of the mean ends up with the highest score, a great deal of admiration, and quite a sense of accomplishment. To top it off, at the professional level, winning involves a sizable purse.

Only the toughest survive in this sport. With a one-ton terror trying to toss and then trample you, you'd best be in top shape. That's why pro riders go through an intense training program, like any other professional athlete.

Just before the cowboy mounts up, the bull is forced into a rectangular chute a tad bigger than the animal. If the creature isn't already steaming with frustration and anger, men standing on the gates of the chute start pulling on his horns and smacking him on the head. If you can believe it, they try to make him even madder than he already was—just seconds before he's released into the rodeo arena. The arena is similar in size to a hockey rink and enclosed by walls to keep the bull out of the spectators' laps.

A leather strap pressed up against his male parts makes the bull kick, stomp, snort, and twist every way possible when the gate opens. And, of course, our cowboy is flailing about like a rag doll, trying to stay on the bull's back during all this mayhem.

Who in his right mind rides these monsters called rodeo bulls? Most bull riders take up the sport during their high school years, looking for an adrenalin rush. If they show promise, some of these crazy cowboys move on to ride on the college-level circuit. And if they're still a little crazy, they try their hand at the professional level, where money is the ultimate reward for a successful eight-second ride.

Rodeo Time!

"Ladies and gentlemen, it's time for tonight's feature event: professional bull riding at its best. Glad you can be with us because tonight will be more exciting than anything you've ever seen. In the chute, mountin' up, is our first rider: Cowboy Brad from Littleton, Texas. This boy is gettin' ready to dance with one of the meanest, toughest, biggest bulls ever, Storm." (Storm is released into the arena, spotlights revealing his enormous bulk and ferocious temper. Music to make the bull angry blares from powerful speakers.)

"Cowboy Brad has driven all the way here from his home in Littleton, craving a shot at riding ol' Storm, the deadliest bull on the planet."

Why would anyone in his right mind want to go head-to-head with a bull, especially one like Storm? No thanks. They can keep their prize money. I'd rather be hunting or doing any number of other things. I don't crave a rush so much that I'm willing to break every bone in my body—or worse. I'll just stay in the stands and watch.

I've never ridden any flesh and blood bulls, but I am well acquainted with the backs of "bulls" nonetheless. My bull-riding exploits do not include climbing on a two-thousand-pound beast—although there are times doing that may have been easier. My Storm riding involves marital issues, child raising, teenage mindreading, economy busting, and family illnesses, among a myriad of other challenges. Then there's that final ride I have yet to take. Death is a storm none of us want to face, but ultimately, we all must get on its back and ride. It's a contest no one can avoid, no matter how hard we try.

One real-life storm that seems to rattle and shake fathers is dealing with their teenage daughters. Those sweet little ladies are the apple of our eye one day and a storm from hell the next. Believe me when I tell you, my daughter was in the champion bull category. I sure tried a lot of mindreading on Candace, but this contest gave me a wild ride on the serious side that nearly trampled me.

Candace Marie Lee

Candace was born August 25, 1986, but her entrance into the world did not afford us time to celebrate. Doctors and nurses immediately noted Candace's troublesome skin color and saw she was barely breathing. With all the skills they could offer and with a sense of urgency, the medical team did everything they could for our little angel. And when they knew her needs were beyond their reach, they rushed her to the local Children's Hospital. A team of newborn specialists immediately went into action. What a nightmare! My wife was still in bed in one hospital and I was at the other with Candace, who was fighting for her very life.

Our new baby survived her battle to be born, but once she was stable and my wife was released from hospital, it was time for that unwanted and unwelcomed task: meeting with Candace's doctor. I will never forget it. This kind, delightful, soft-spoken doctor asked us into his office and invited us to sit. Words could not come out of my wife's mouth fast enough. She drilled him with question after question: "What's wrong with my baby? What are you going to do about it? When will she get better?" Most of all, Rhonda wanted to know when we could take our daughter home.

There's something about a mother's love we men can't grasp. Dads try, but a mother feels and hurts, laughs and cries for her children in a way only God Himself can relate to. I say this with a broken heart, crying as I write: Men, when a mother hurts for her children, even if you don't understand why, you must stop everything. And I mean stop because your wife needs you in those moments like in no others. Be willing to eat dirt you may or may not deserve. Be willing to be silent, even if your mouth wants to speak. Open your arms and your heart. Get them wide open and embrace your hurting spouse with everything you can. Don't walk in front of her—come up humbly beside her. Hold her when she's weak and catch her if she starts to fall.

Men, when a woman hurts for her child, you need to be there. Golf, fishing, and Friday night out with the guys are all out the window during those times. When a storm of life hits your kids, know that Mom is part of that storm, whether she wants to be or not.

Clearly, calmly, and with all the care he could give, the doctor explained the situation. "Mr. and Mrs. Lee, Candace has a heart condition known as tricuspid atresia." (We couldn't even pronounce it, much less understand what it was.) "Your baby doesn't have a right ventricle. She's living with only half of her heart functioning."

We were stunned. "So what do we do?"

He explained that until just a short time before, babies with Candace's condition didn't live, and if they did, it was usually for less than two years.

A bull ride began we weren't prepared for. My wife screamed, then cried uncontrollably. I wept too. My heart didn't know where to go first. I didn't know if I was crying with pain for our little baby girl or with a level of hurt I'd never felt before from watching my bride completely lose her composure. Both occurred as I sat there helplessly. Rhonda was screaming in torment, and our little girl two floors up fighting moment by moment, breath by breath, for her life. Yes, this storm immediately became the storm of all storms for us. Little did we know how much bull riding we were about to do over the coming years.

Despite her limitations, Candace Marie became one of the all-time champion bull riders herself. No storm was ever too big or strong, never mean enough that she couldn't ride the eternal eight seconds. As worried parents, we were forever asking the doctors, who were among the best of the best, "What are her limitations?"

"Whatever her body tells her."

"How long does she have?"

"As long as her heart says so."

Because of muscle damage around the heart, she was not a transplant candidate.

How did Candace live the next twenty-two years? She grew up bull riding, skydiving, and Rocky Mountain climbing until she breathed her last breath. Rollercoasters one day, zip lining the next. If she was able, Candace did it.

She looked normal most days, so few people knew she was dying. She moved to Florida and worked at Disney World for six months while going to their Disney business school. She went horseback riding in Wyoming, snorkeling in Aruba, hot-air ballooning in Yellowstone, and four-wheeling in Upper Michigan. She drove snowmobiles like a demon, bowled like a pro, and danced every silly dance she could come up with. Candace went to school to be a pharmaceutical tech, helped Dad in the office, went to church every week, and was simply on the go as much as her body would allow.

Yes, there were many times when the heart said, "Slow down, Candace, I need a break." And we rushed her to the hospital on a regular basis. But no matter what storm came her way, she simply jumped on its back and held on for the ride. She never asked for sympathy and never told people what she was going through. Just like the bull-riding cowboy, she got up on the beast's back all by herself and rode just as hard and for just as long as she could. She rode until the eight-second horn signaling eternity sounded just after midnight on May 19, 2009.

The Last Ride

During the winter of 2008–2009, my wife's parents decided to go on a cruise for their golden wedding anniversary. They wanted both daughters and their families to join them in their celebration. (You may remember that 2008 was "a year from hell" economically.) Being in small business, taking a cruise didn't seem to be the wisest move. But with family support, some pleading from the kids, and a few business blessings from God—yes, God loves a working man—we pulled together the resources to go on this adventure. Our destination? The islands of Hawaii.

My in-laws were going all out. Far from being wealthy, they'd been saving their pennies for years. This was going to be a once-in-a-lifetime experience—and something even more dramatic for our dear Candace.

The plane was scheduled to leave Saturday morning, May 15, 2009, but someone forgot to tell Candace's heart she was heading to Hawaii. The day before, at 11:00 in the morning, I rushed Candace from my office—she worked with me when her health allowed—to Detroit Children's Hospital. The usual twenty-minute trip took us twelve.

Candace had gone into tachycardia, which meant her heart was racing at an unbelievable rate. Candace's heart was pumping at over 200 beats per minute, which she often said made her feel as though someone had driven a car onto her chest. We rushed into emergency as we had probably over a hundred times before. There an expert team of some of the medical field's best was standing by. We had gone through this exercise so many times over the years that most of the staff, regardless of their shift, knew our angel by name and why she was coming in.

The team began to do their thing: check here, inject there, move over there. Out came the paddles to zap her heart and the IV started to flow. Rhonda had arrived, and the two of us began to pray as we'd prayed thousands of times before: "O God, please watch over our baby just one more time. Please God, slow her heart down and let her get better."

While the medical team, as well as the parents, were going crazy, there was our bull rider, weighing a whopping 115 pounds, sitting up in the bed saying, "Hey now, wait just a minute. I can't stay here. I can't be sick. I have a plane to catch tomorrow. I'm going on a cruise."

As a resident checked this and a doctor checked that, it appeared that once again God had given Candace another day of life. After a few hours of extreme care, our bull rider said these exact words: "I'm outta here!" The medical team agreed her numbers looked normal—for her. Her color was better and she seemed to be breathing fine. Since she was over eighteen, they couldn't make her stay.

Our determined, pistol-packing daughter was so serious about leaving, she grabbed the IV tubes and with fire in her eyes stated, "Look, I'm going out with some friends tonight and I have a plane to catch in the morning. So either you pull out this IV or I will!" (I can assure you she meant it.)

Sure as shootin', on Saturday our families, Candace

included, took off as scheduled for our trip to Paradise. "Hawaiian Islands, here we come!"

Monster Bull Ride

Almost as soon as we boarded the ship, it became obvious our tough little bull rider was not up to her normal self. She was pale, vomiting, short of breath, and needed even more rest than normal.

By the time we reached the first port, Candace was already so sick she couldn't go on any planned excursions. So we waved down a cab and I told the driver we'd like him to take us—Candace, her brother, Jeromy, and me—on a private tour. I explained that Candace was not feeling well and that we had rented a wheelchair for her aboard ship. I asked him to show us as much as he could and yet make it as easy as possible for Candace to get around. With dollar signs dancing in his eyes and a soft smile, this taxi driver became our tour guide for most of the day.

We did some shopping, which Candace loved. She bought a watercolor picture of a butterfly. She loved the beauty of butterflies. She wasn't into the big ticket items, just little pieces here and there. We saw some tremendous parks and waterfalls. On the other side of the island, I took one of the final pictures of my baby girl.

The next day her mom, grandpa, and grandma took Candace out touring again. They went to an aquarium. She loved animals of any kind, so this was right up her alley. Once again, family pushed her in the wheelchair. She simply didn't have the strength to walk.

During these few days, everyone in the family was keeping a close watch on Candace. We had the ship's medical staff treating her and checking in from time to time as well. On the evening of the eighteenth, we all dined together, but Candace felt so bad she went back to her cabin to lie down. After dinner, the rest of the family went to see a show, but I went to check up on her. I found her in terrible condition, so I got Rhonda and we took her straight to the doctors.

We could tell Candace was fading. The medical staff was doing everything they could to get an IV flowing but with no success. We were at sea and could only hope to make it to the next port, where we could take her to the nearest hospital.

Candace was in terrible pain. Her remaining color was fading. As she slipped further from us, she screamed, "I can't take this anymore." Those were the last words I heard my baby girl say.

After the ship's medical team worked on her for over two hours, the doctor came out and said, "I'm sorry. We've done all we can. I have to call it."

At the sweet age of twenty-two, our daughter was dead. She was gone forever from our lives.

Do you ever feel as though one storm after another is crashing upon you? Do you ever feel as if the hailstones of life are just too much to handle? Ever feel tired, lonely, and abandoned? Tornados, lightning, and disasters come at some point regardless of who you are. It's not *if* the hail is going to fall but how you handle it when it does. God has not forsaken you. He's closer than you may realize. Our God, the Lord Almighty, doesn't fail. Remember Job? There's hope. I know.

Paul: Bull Riding for Jesus

Let's take a look at Paul, perhaps one of God's best recruits, who turned out to be a champion bull rider. Our friend Paul dealt with hurricanes, floods, and whirlwinds. You name the bull and he rode it. As with Job, I'm confident you'll recognize your own situation in at least some of his.

Saul of Tarsus came on the scene in the book of Acts not long after Jesus had been crucified, rose, and then ascended back to heaven. Saul was a Jew who had clout with the local leadership. He hated everything Jesus represented, and he hated anyone who claimed to be His follower. Acts 8 says Saul and an approved army of men started going everywhere, persecuting and imprisoning anyone claiming Jesus Christ as the Son of God.

With mean and evil intent, Saul was on his way south to Damascus when lightning struck and he fell to the ground. But God had other plans, and while traveling to Damascus, He put powerful and mighty Saul on his first bull.

Lightning struck. Saul fell to the ground. God spoke. (Remember, when God speaks, we would be extremely wise to listen.) Saul lost his sight for a few days. Then God sent a man named Ananias to pray for him. Saul's sight was restored. He was no longer Saul the killer of Christians, but Paul, the one who would lay down his life for his belief in the Son of God.

Saul was the meanest of the mean. He had clout and power. Everything a man could want, Saul had. His shoulders were covered with the worst of sins. However, God in His master plan said, "Hey, Saul, put aside your plans for the rest of your life for I've called you out. You're no longer going to harm my people. You're going to help them."

I can hear God speaking rodeo style. "Paul, my man, you'd better get your cowboy hat and boots on. You need to buy the best rope possible because you're about to ride some of the meanest and baddest bulls anywhere on the planet. Get ready!"

Once Paul submitted to God's plan, I wonder then if he

really knew what he had gotten himself into. I can hear him saying, "Thank you, God. You've opened my mind and eyes to you. Yes, God, I'll be more than happy to tell others about you and your plan for their lives. No problem. I'll travel all over the world speaking your name. Seems simple enough, so why isn't everyone doing this?" Little did Paul know just how many bull rides he would need to take.

You may think Paul was some kind of heavenly saint from the beginning. He wasn't. Yes, he was called by God for His purpose. True, the Holy Spirit dwelled within him and directed his life. But all in all, Paul was still just a man like you and me.

Although called as a missionary and church planter, Paul still had just as many daily struggles as the rest of us. For the most part, he got up every Monday morning and went to work. He was a tentmaker by trade. I'm confident he had his share of family issues. He had ongoing confrontations with others who were also followers of Jesus. Don't think for a moment that because God called him everything was going to be smooth sailing. His adventure was anything but rosy.

During and after work, Paul presented the message of Jesus Christ to all who would listen. When Saturday came, he rushed to the synagogue and waited patiently to challenge legalistic Jews about all sorts of matters. On Sunday, he went to where the people lived, to their local churches, teaching and encouraging them in their faith.

And what was Paul's earthly reward? In Acts 16, we see Paul and his co-worker Silas stripped, battered, and jailed. Chapter 21 tells us Paul was dragged and beaten. Why? For declaring the word of the Lord. He was then bound with not one but two chains and arrested. You'll also find in Acts 23 that a group of religious people took an oath and plotted to kill our brother Paul. He was on trial before Felix, falsely accused of stirring up riots. And as if all this weren't enough, he went from one beating to another before Festus. How many trials does a man have to go through simply for speaking the truth and living a righteous life?

Later as Paul sailed to Rome, a hurricane smashed the ship he was on (Acts 27). The broken boat drifted about for some fourteen days and finally ran aground on an island called Malta. Remember, Paul was a prisoner during this time, not a tourist on a vacation cruise.

Wow! Paul has to be up there with the greatest bull-riding champions of all time. His bucking bulls came daily, one after another after another until finally, he rode that beast called Death for his Savior right into heaven.

Paul's Training Program

What was the secret of Paul's strength? How did he keep going? Well, after that first flash of light, he walked with Jesus. More correctly, Jesus walked with him and in him by way of the Holy Spirit. The two of them were always riding and wrestling the storms of life together.

Paul put a positive spin on every situation he found himself in. Arrested and put in jail? He sang, preached, and praised. Shipwrecked with his captors? He helped them get safely to land. Mocked by his jailers for his message of Christ? He gave thanks that the gospel was still being preached—even if by hypocrites.

Rewards? The apostle Paul has much to say about prizewinning. He speaks about our lowly bodies being conformed to the glorious body of the King of kings and Lord of lords, our Savior, Jesus Christ. We'll be in heaven with our God, our Friend, forever. Now that, my friends, is a prize worth everything we can give. For every believer who gives his all, God will say, "Well done, my good and faithful servant. Enter in for your reward" (Matthew 25:23 paraphrased). Isn't this what this life is all about, preparing us for the next one, for all eternity?

If there is anything to be learned from the bull rides of life, it's this: Life isn't always fair. But when one bull bucks you off, get up and climb on again. And when the next bull attempts to throw you, hang on just a little tighter. Seek the Word of God for wisdom and knowledge. Paul did. Be a successful sufferer. Hold tightly to the rope of faith with a little more spiritual rosin. Put your indwelling Holy Spirit cowboy hat back on. Ride the storms of life for all you're worth because, as Paul says, there's a prize waiting when all the rides are over.

Our Lord knew what it was to ride the orneriest of bulls. He left the perfection of heaven to be born in a barn. He led an ordinary childhood in a humble home . . . well, "ordinary" except for fleeing to Egypt and returning to the out-of-the-way community of Nazareth because the king wanted Him dead. He had a three-year ministry surrounded by disciples who didn't fully understand His mission and crowds who wanted most of all to have their physical needs met. The final bull ride involved being falsely accused, beaten, and crucified for crimes He didn't commit. Those crimes? Our sins. The good news is that He stayed aboard, not for a few seconds—or even a few minutes. He rode the bull all the way to death. Then He rose victorious over the ornery bull of this life to win the victory not for Himself—but for us!

We Are Bull Riders Too

Are there mountains in front of you? God will help you

scale the Everests in your life, but you do have to climb. God doesn't just bungee you over the mountains. With His help, you can ride out the eight seconds that sometimes seem to last forever. He's right there for the next bull you have to get on, and rest assured, there is another one coming. He leads you on your adventures. Then whether you live to be one hundred or only twenty-two, know that you lived life to its fullest. You were always in God's hands.

Our daughter, Candace, didn't use her physical condition as an excuse for not living life to the fullest. No, she climbed up on the back of one bull or another every day. If she fell one day, she'd get up and try again the next. She knew there were situations one has to ride out. They don't magically go away. They may never go away. Hang onto that rope as tightly as you can, and trust God with everything you have. He's not in the failing business.

"In this world you will have trouble. But take heart! I have overcome the world" (John 16:33). That's why Jesus came. He knew we would have struggles. He knew there would be bulls to ride. But here's the great news: Jesus Himself gives us His strength to ride them. We are His children and He takes care of his own. He is God Almighty.

Here's the straight scoop: God gives us hope and wisdom beyond measure when we ask, but ultimately, we need to remember we are created for His purpose and not ours. We must get our priorities straight. We shouldn't expect God's blessings if our focus is on ourselves and not on Him.

Maybe your marriage is on the edge. Maybe life together hasn't been as rosy as you dreamed it would be. Men, love your wives as Christ loved the church. Jesus loves the church unconditionally. He died for it. He offers grace for our imperfections. If Christ, the Lord of Lords, can do that for us, surely we can do the same in our marriages.

Don't like your job? Show me in the Bible where God says He'll make sure you have the perfect place to work. No, He says to get up, work with your hands, let the peace of God dwell within you, and let your light shine to those around you. God never promised the perfect occupation, but He did say, "Never will I leave you; never will I forsake you" (Hebrews 13:5). When you trust in God for every need, when you humble yourself so His will can be accomplished in you, you can bet the Almighty will be with you no matter where you're working or what you're doing.

Money problems got you down? Whose handiwork was this? Yours perhaps? Did you buy more than you could afford? Did the pride of life get you in trouble? Maybe you weren't talking to God enough for guidance with your finances. Although it may look grim and there appears to be no hope to pay the bills, fall to your knees, pray, and listen. Listen to what the Holy Spirit speaks in your heart. Give attention to the Word of God. Don't let the world's ideas scare you or lead you down a wrong path. Our God never fails.

Not doing well raising the kids? Are you leading them by example or only by what you say? Great leaders go out in front and show others how it's done. Are you a yeller? Then your kids will yell back. Is grounding your solution for every disciplinary need? They'll eventually run away just as fast and as far as they can. Use the rod of correction when need be. Seek wisdom continually. And most of all, love unconditionally.

Have you lost a loved one? Can't seem to move on with your life because you are forever dwelling on theirs? Jesus said the dead should take care of the dead. Think this is crude? Ask me as I fight with Candace's death on a regular basis. When

Candace died, I was flat on the ground, face down, with the bull on top. But I ran to Jesus, and He picked me up. Depressed? Sure. In anguish? Of course. Did it take time? You bet. But I got back on the bull anyway and here I am. It still hurts, but God is on the throne and He has work for me to do. I know she's in glory, but I still miss her every day. I realize the best thing I can do is to live my life for Jesus, assuring myself of the hope I will see her again soon.

Don't dwell on those "shoulda-coulda-woulda" things of the past. Dwell on living your life as if there's no tomorrow because tomorrow never comes. Lift your head toward heaven, give the God of gods your praise, seek His blessings and direction each day, and get ready for another bull ride. Don't let Satan keep you in the dirt. That is not God's way. Get all your equipment and gear on, climb back up on those bulls of life, and ride. With God's help, you will be amazed by how many successful eight-second rides you'll have.

Jesus was the ultimate bull rider. And, like our daughter Candace, His life was short and to the point. Every breath He took and every move He made were done with purpose and meaning. Our Savior's bull ride was on an old wooden cross where He bore our sins, where He gave His life so you and I could be saved from eternal separation from His father God.

But thankfully, He rode His bull for that eight eternal seconds and even longer. His bull, the cross, could not keep Him down, for by the power of God in Him and by the authority of heaven, the stone of His grave was rolled away and He was not inside. He arose! Praise God! Our Lord and Savior lives forevermore. Because He lives, you and I can ride any storm of life out there. Yes, because of Jesus, there is no bull too mean, too big, too powerful to overcome what Jesus did for us on the cross.

In Summary

Jesus was—and still is—the perfect bull rider and best living example for us today.

- He studied the words of the prophets. We must study God's Word, the Bible.

- He often prayed long and hard to His Father.

- He prepared Himself with godly wisdom before temptations came or the enemy tried to deceive Him.

- He made every day count and filled each one with purpose.

- He had complete faith in His Heavenly Father.

- There was never a bull named Storm or called by any other name that was too much for Him because His Father lived in Him.

- He rode the ultimate bull and scored the biggest prize of all: the washing away of our sins.

Jesus wants you and me to be great bull riders as well.

Consider this . . .

1. Think about one of the roughest bull rides you've had. Were you a successful sufferer? Why or why not?

2. Think of some of your tough times. Describe at least one good thing that came from one or more of them.

3. Describe a mountain looming in your path right now. Think about this: Is the mountain blocking *your* path for your life—or *God's* path? If it's your path, are you willing to give up your plans and submit to His? If it's His path, will you trust Him to help you climb the mountain? What steps are you willing to take to build your faith?

Chapter 3

I Got One!

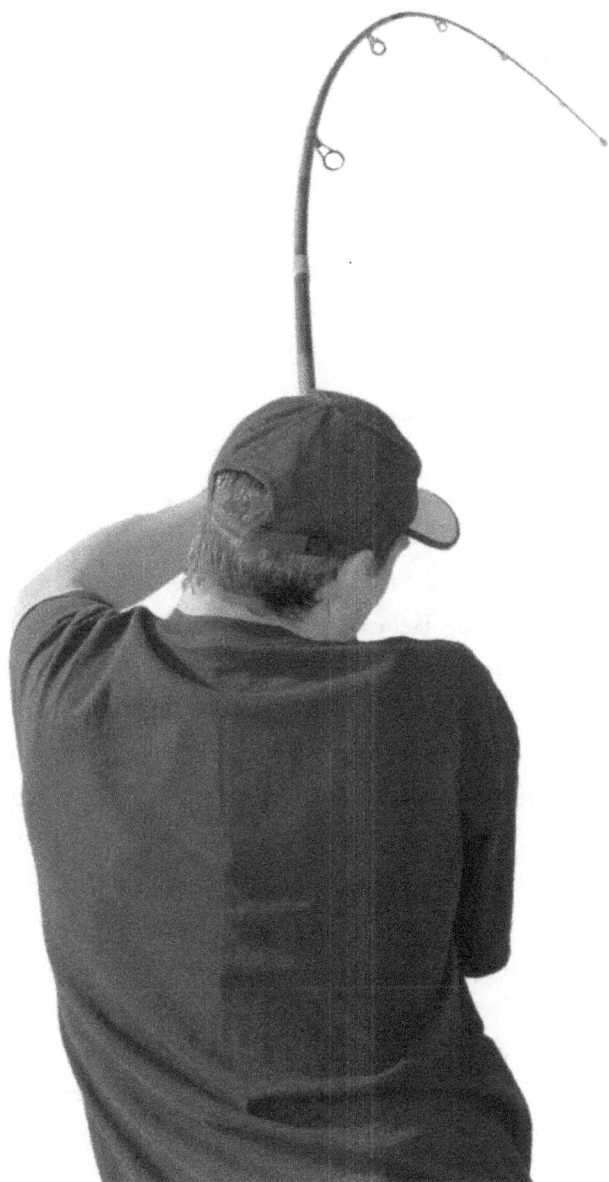

"I GOT ONE! I GOT ONE!"

"Hold onto it. Don't let go! Make sure your hook is set!"

"I can't hold on much longer. He's a big one! . . . Oh darn! He broke my line!"

Ever hooked into "the big one"? Ever had the fight of your life with a fish? Believe me, I've tried many times, but sport fishing and me just ain't buddy buddy. I've been on my share of professional charters and, as they say, struck out. I've owned fishing boats equipped with the latest and greatest in fish-finding equipment, and the results were still the same—zip. I've even tried my hand fishing at those fish farms and still came up with the smallest one in the water. After years of trying, my dreams of catching the Big One have all but faded.

Still, I want to share one quick fish story with you. Some years back, our family decided to take a little vacation. As part of our adventure, we bought Jeromy and Candace, who were four and six at the time, Disney fishing rods and reels. Along with all our other gear, we packed these highly advanced poles in our trunk, piled into the minivan, and headed north to what is called "Yooper country," Michigan's Upper Peninsula.

We'd been on our summer slam just two days when we came across a spot by Black River where a bunch of people along the bank and a few anglers in boats had dropped their lines.

"Whoo hoo, Dad! Can we stop and fish?" the kids yelled.

I sized up the situation and turned into a gravel parking lot. We hopped out, grabbed the kids' super duper fishing gear, and headed for the bank. The bait? Hot dogs from the cooler. Tackle? One hook and one bobber for each rod.

Jeromy was so excited he was about to pee his pants. Just like his daddy, he couldn't wait to catch that big fish. With a little bit of a stutter he said, "C-c-a-n I d-d-dooooo i-i-i-ttt, D-d-d-aaa-d-e-e-e?"

His mother yelled, "Jeromy, do you need to go potty?"

"N-no, M-m-mom."

"Well, why are you holding yourself?"

Just before he wet himself, his mom hurried him behind the van door and told him to do his thing.

Meanwhile, pro fisherwoman Candace and I had already cast our lines, looking for the Big One. Finally after Jeromy took care of business, he too lobbed his lure into the drink, anticipating a whopper "as big as our van" to jump onto his hook.

While we toiled away on the bank, we noticed a couple of guys out on the lake having problems getting their boat back to the ramp, some sort of engine trouble. They eventually had to paddle their way back to shore, but that scene was temporarily forgotten because of something far more exciting.

Candace screamed, "I GOT ONE!"

"Got what?"

"I got a fish!"

And what a fish! If I hadn't seen it with my own eyes, I

wouldn't have believed it. Sure enough, hooked onto the end of my six-year-old's pole was a monster-size northern muskie. I too almost peed my pants.

"Reel, Candace, reel! Pull with all your might!"

"I can't do it anymore, Daddy! I'm too tired. You gotta help me."

While we wrestled the whopper next to the bank, I realized we had nothing to get it out of the water with. It was that big. And northerns have razor-sharp teeth and are not selective about whom they use them on.

As Moby Muskie came along shore, people began crowding around, eyes wide. An elderly man and his wife—who appeared to have had more success with their drinking than their fishing—sidled up. "I'll tell you what," he said. "I'll get the fish out of the water for you, clean it, and cut it up in fillets if you'll split it with us."

That sounded good to me since that fish wasn't going anywhere otherwise.

However, just before they began slicing and dicing, a young guy said, "Wait a minute. You need to go to the DNR (Department of Natural Resources) and have this fish measured and weighed before you clean it. I think it could be a record."

No sooner had he finished speaking than a DNR officer pulled up. I hurried over and asked him to take a look at the fish.

"Yep, it might be," he said after checking it over, "except for one thing. This fish appears to have been hit by a boat prop." He pointed to a long gash in the whale's belly.

Remember the guys with the engine problem?

Well, Candace and her fish didn't make it into the record books after all. But it was still a good day to go fishing and a great day for our family.

The Big Fisherman

What about it? Got any good fish stories to tell? Ever hooked into the Big One yourself? Know anyone who has the touch for catching fish?

How about Simon Peter, one of Jesus' disciples? He was a fisherman by trade. It's one thing to fish for fun but doing it for a living? Did you know that for years now commercial fishing has been ranked as one of the top ten most dangerous occupations in the world? This is not a job for the faint of heart or weak of body. Just as Candace and I found out, it takes work to haul in those smelly, floppy animals.

Let's take a closer look at the life of our guy, Simon Peter the fisherman. Some argue he was a rough and tough loudmouth. Others say he was full of love and compassion. I believe he was both. Whichever side you take, know this: Peter was a working man, just like you and me.

Peter was a commercial fisherman. He worked with his brother, Andrew, and their business partners, the brothers James and John. Peter was a hardworking small business owner. He had partner issues, overhead, and responsibility for payroll. It was up to him to keep the boats in good working order. He made sure the taxes were paid and was the first one on the boat every morning.

After a long, hard day at sea, it was Peter who still had to help clean the catch and then hurry it to the market to be sold. Some days were rough as they had little gain for all their hard work. Other times, the catch was very rewarding but still involved dangerous physical work and long hours.

The Bible tells us this hardworking, everyday guy and his brother were the first disciples Jesus called to follow Him. Of all the accounts in the Bible, Peter's story paints one of the most amazing scenes. Jesus, the Son of God, came to earth. He was sent by our heavenly Father as both the example and the path to eternal hope in glory. He was born to a young virgin through the power of the Holy Spirit. His earthly dad was like a stepfather. Jesus was raised as a carpenter's son and, some argue, may have attended rabbi school until the age of twenty-nine or thirty. At thirty, Jesus began public ministry. He devoted His time and attention to a ragtag bunch. After three and a half brief years, these twelve were equipped to reach the world with the knowledge that Jesus is the living hope for our eternity.

Since Jesus was going to use these men for the most important purpose in history, sharing the message of real hope, you'd think He would choose the elite. It would stand to reason the Lord would want men knowledgeable in the Old Testament. They would need to be good public speakers because they would be the ones to deliver the Good News throughout the world.

Supposing Jesus would only look for the best in His hiring process, you would think these guys would be the smartest of the smart from only the finest families. You'd think all this, right? But what Jesus did simply blows me away.

Peter and Andrew and at least one other crew—likely James and John—had been out fishing. They were there, but the fish weren't. It was one of those pre-dawn, cold morning starts, and they were hoping to hit the fish jackpot, but all they got for their efforts were a few minnows.

There they were, on the shore, cleaning their nets—tired, frustrated, and just wanting to go home and crash. But Jesus had other plans for these dirt-digging, fish-finding guys.

I can hear Jesus now. "Okay, guys, I'm done talking for now. I'll tell you what. Why don't you paddle these boats out into deeper water? My heavenly fish finder tells me there are a lot of fish right over there about 200 yards."

Of course, these men had no idea who Jesus really was. They had no knowledge of His greatness or power. None of them knew He was the Son of God, the promised Messiah. Even so, they said, "If you say so, we'll give it a chance. I mean, it's been such a rotten day for fishing anyhow. What have we got to lose?"

They reached the place Jesus pointed out, let down the nets, and caught more fish than they could haul in their boat. Peter was in awe. Once back on shore, he fell to his knees and said to Jesus, "Go away from me Lord, for I am a sinful man." As though Jesus didn't already know this about him!

But Jesus said to this foul-mouthed, smelly, grumpy, small business owning, normal working stiff, commercial fisherman, "Nope, I'm not going away from you, Peter. In fact, I want you to give up your fishing business because I want to spend the next three and a half years pouring into you everything I can about eternal kingdom fishing. You, Peter, shall be a fisher for men's everlasting souls. Your name as well as your works will be spoken of and followed after for many generations to come."

These guys weren't members of the rich and famous club. Jesus handpicked working men to lead the world to Himself. Just think. Jesus handed the most important mission in history to four hardworking, sunup-to-sundown, often bad attitude fishermen. Jesus picked them. And He picked you and me.

Let's look a little longer at Peter's life. We already know Peter was a fisherman by trade. We also know he had a wife, since Jesus healed his mother-in-law (Luke 4:38). Peter had a lot in common with many of us. He had a wife, a mother-in-law, and perhaps children. There's also a good chance he had a father-in-law and other family as well. In all likelihood, Peter had to deal with family challenges as well as run the business. Need I say more? Can you relate?

This same Peter was a leader. Repeatedly in the New Testament, we see Peter leading the way—sometimes with his words, sometimes with words coupled with actions. Peter had a Type A personality. Whatever he set out to do, he did. And if he told his workers and partners to do something, they did it.

Don't think because Jesus called Peter to be one of the so-called elite twelve that his mouth and actions didn't get him into trouble from time to time. In fact, he was usually drowning in more hot water than the rest of the disciples. He cut off the ear of a guy when they came to arrest Jesus. He chewed out Jesus for wanting to wash his feet during the Last Supper. He even bragged he'd never leave Jesus, then denied—not once, but three times—that he ever knew Him.

If you're a man, you are called to be a leader in one way or another. A true leader is humble, tender, kind, teachable, loveable, and giving of time and things. An awesome leader never tells others he's a leader—those around him will simply be drawn to follow him. Jesus was and still is the greatest leader of all time. We would all do well to lead like Jesus.

As a small business owner, I can relate to Peter more than I'd like to admit. Here's a sample of my leadership: "Come on guys, let's pick it up. You're dragging on me. Lunch? You want lunch after the slow, lazy work you've done this morning? You want to stop for half an hour and eat your lunch? Are you crazy? Are you trying to get fired?"

Or maybe someone else came up with a good idea. Me, being downright dumb, would reply, "Well, okay, Joe, thanks for your thoughts, but I want it done *this* way," as though I never heard anything he said.

Have you done any of the dumb things Peter and I have done? Do you boss your wife around instead of communicating gently with her? What about the kids, especially the older ones? Are you talking *to* them or are you talking *at* them? Are you open to what they have to say or is there just a tunnel from ear to ear with everything blowing straight through? Is it your way or the highway? Are you always right, even when you're 100 percent wrong? Do you lead your wife and family with the love of Christ, or do Internet sites, newspapers, the people you work with, and TV dictate your walk in this world?

While I'm at it, allow me to address the subject of our surroundings. We all know Jesus selected twelve men to surround Him. We also know they came from some pretty rough and tumble backgrounds. They weren't exactly saint material when Jesus took them in. However, He was able to plant in them the message of eternal hope. He taught and showed them firsthand the love, grace, power, and forgiveness offered to them by the God of the universe.

The point I want you to get is this: Jesus surrounded Himself with a bunch of normal guys just like you and me. Ordinary guys would take the gospel message throughout the world.

You and I become part of our environment every day. No matter how tough you think you are, your surroundings impact everything in your life. For example, if you work all the time with a bunch of guys who have foul mouths, eventually, it'll rub off on you. If you're not careful, this will happen more often than you may think.

Drinking? Start going to the local watering hole with the gang after work before going home, and soon you're spending your paycheck pounding down one drink after another. Before you know it, your drinking friends have become your family advisors, your accountants, your lawyers—your everything. And they have all the answers too. All these great words of guidance coming from people who can't legally drive themselves home.

Listen to off-color jokes? Don't kid yourself. They're not just off-color; they're downright dirty, filthy stories. The same goes for stories that put down or make fun of others. They make us feel good and cover up our own hurts and failures. The more we're surrounded by these jokes and stupid talk, the more we become just like the hurting, unrighteous men telling them. You can rest assured God is not laughing with you.

Change Is Only a Choice Away

I could go on and on, but I hope by now you get the message. Every man is called to be a leader, and we should lead God's way. Peter was once an ungodly leader, but when he met the Savior, our man began to change into a real working man. He became a great example of a true leader. Jesus had seen beyond what Peter was and focused on what he would become.

After Jesus returned to heaven and His Holy Spirit came on those folks who were in that room in Jerusalem, Peter went out and spoke the truth about his Master to thousands. He was tossed into prison and taken before rulers for speaking the truth. Years later, according to tradition, he was crucified like his Lord for spreading the good news. Along the way, he had some growing up to do, but he followed Jesus to his eternal hope.

Read these words Peter himself wrote near the end of his life:

"Love one another deeply, from the heart" (1 Peter 1:22).

50

"Live in harmony with one another. . . . Do not be conceited" (Romans 12:16).

"Love each other deeply, because love covers over a multitude of sins" (1 Peter 4:8).

"Clothe yourselves with humility toward one another" (1 Peter 5:5).

"Grow in the grace and knowledge of our Lord and Savior Jesus Christ" (2 Peter 3:18).

Love. Harmony. Compassion. Humility. This was not the "before" Peter speaking; it was the "after" Peter. After Jesus poured Himself into Peter, the disciple began to love people and then set his line to catch men—not fish—for the rest of his life.

The Big One

For our thirty-first anniversary, my wife and I spent part of the day hanging out along the St. Clair River. It was an absolutely perfect day, sunny with a light breeze from the west. As we sat in our lawn chairs reading together and just reminiscing about our life together, three children were trying their hand at fishing. They got a few nibbles now and again but couldn't seem to hook anything.

Then one of them handed the rod over to another young gal and said, "Throw it way out there as far as you can so we can catch the big one."

The Big One. Did those words ever ring in my head! Isn't that exactly what Jesus is telling us all to do? Cast your line "way out there." Take a risk once in a while. Live by faith. Work hard. Be willing to walk on water for His name's sake. Isn't this the way Jesus wants us to live? Sure it is. We must exercise godly wisdom and knowledge with a sense of letting God walk in front, leading the way, not trailing in the dust somewhere behind us.

Throw your line out as far as you can to lead a friend or loved one to the saving knowledge of our Lord Jesus. Cast that rod as hard as you can to lift up a drowning friend suffering loneliness or pain.

The one little gal said something else that hit me right between the eyes. "Let's put a big juicy worm on the hook so we catch the biggest fish possible."

Oh my! Out of the mouth of babes! That young girl's words reminded me of what Jesus said in Matthew 28:19: "Go and make disciples of all nations." Our Lord's greatest command came just before He returned to His heavenly Father. "Go and tell everyone you can about me; both my promises and my eternal hope for those who will follow after me. Go! Use the best and biggest bait you can. Invite them over for dinner. Visit someone in the hospital who has no visitors. Take hold of the drug or alcohol abuser and love all over him."

Go ahead. Cast your lines and catch the knowledge of who Jesus is and what He wants you to do. Snag a wife who will walk by your side and become your partner in the fishing for men and women business. Land a job where you can provide for your family, where you can catch more fish and use your earnings to train other fishermen around the world. Reel in a family that will be a lighthouse in your neighborhood.

It may not be today or even tomorrow, but when you use the best worms, the juicy ones, eventually—like those children fishing—you'll be able to say, "I got one! I got a big one! For His glory, my God used me to reach the down-and-outer. He used me, a blatant sinner, as bait to reach the outcast and the lost."

My Father, who art in Heaven, let me catch a big one today for your glory.

In Summary

- Jesus doesn't necessarily choose the elite to accomplish His purposes. "But God chose the foolish things of the world to shame the wise; God chose the weak things of the world to shame the strong" (1 Corinthians 1:27). We don't have to be the richest, the smartest, or the best looking to be of service to Him.

- We just may see amazing things happen when we obey God's instructions—even when they don't make sense, like going back into the deep water after an unsuccessful night of fishing.

- Facing God's awesome power should cause us to humble ourselves before Him. He is no more willing to leave us alone than He was Peter. Jesus wants to be there with us every minute of every day, accomplishing in and through us far more than we ever imagined.

- As men, we are leaders—but that doesn't mean we have to be dictators. We must study how Jesus led His followers and, with His help, learn from His example.

- God wants to use us to catch the Big One. And when we do, He wants us to go right back out there, bait our hook, and go after another.

Consider this . . .

1. What kind of leader are you in your home? What kind of leader would you like to be in your home? Any differences? List steps you will take, starting this week, to become a better leader.

2. Describe what kind of leader you are among people you know. Are you the kind of leader who is likely to catch fish—for Jesus? Name at least one step you will take to become a better fisher of men.

Chapter 4

Open Mouth Insert Boot

"Good morning, Pastor Stacey. Great message! It would have been one of your best if it hadn't been so long." *Ouch!*

"Way to go, Pastor Tony. Fantastic service today, but the music was too loud. Think you can have them turn it down next week?" *Hmm!*

"Rhonda sweetheart, about dinner . . . The steak was a little rare. The baked potato was too hard. And the rolls weren't warm enough. But overall, not a bad meal."

"As your father, I'm not letting you out of the house in *that* get-up."

"Hey there, my dear son, Jeromy, great game today— even though you didn't get a hit the entire game. You really shouldn't have missed that fly ball, you know. And why in the world didn't you throw it to the cut-off man? You cost your team some runs on that one. But other than those screw-ups, you did okay, son."

Gee, thanks for all the encouragement, Dad. Can't wait to return the favor someday.

"Encourage one another," the Bible says. It doesn't tell us to beat one another into the ground. Yet, so often—many times without even thinking (which is part of the problem)— we open our months just long and wide enough to stick our boot-clad foot straight in.

Even when I have nothing but good intentions, so often I find the way I say things ends up doing more harm than good. I know I'm not alone in this. Take our kids for example. "Don't do as I do; do as I say." Ever cheat on your taxes, sell a lemon while claiming the truck was in "great shape," yell at your wife for spending too much on clothes without thinking twice about buying a new hunting rifle? Now, if that's not putting your boot square in your mouth, I don't know what is.

Fathers and Their Kids

How do you talk to your children? What words come out of your mouth for their ears to hear? Our kids hear every word we say, even when we think they're not listening. They also see what we're doing, even when we don't think they're watching.

The way we talk to our kids impacts their walk on this earth. Make your son feel like a loser by slamming him down often enough, and before you know it, he may be living on the streets or, worse yet, seeing life from behind bars. Tell a daughter she dresses like a prostitute, and before you know it, she just might be working the streets.

Too drastic? Have you seen the stats? One out of five teen girls puts nude photos of themselves on the Internet. Fifty percent of girls between fifteen and nineteen have participated in oral sex. The average age for girls to have sex is seventeen. Shocking? It should be. And guess what . . . 63 percent of all girls wish their parents would talk straight with them about sex and other important matters.[1]

Dare to ask a thirteen-year-old boy about life. Ask him what he knows about sex, drugs, and violence. Add to that list what he knows about drinking, partying, stealing, and scamming others. Dads, keep your eyes and ears wide open. Today's kids are exposed to everything, and I do mean *everything*. "Oh, not mine," you say? Look no further than TV, movies, books, YouTube, and various other sites on the Web.

Paul cautioned Timothy, "People will be lovers of themselves" (2 Timothy 3:2). (As I've mentioned before, it's all about me, me, me.) They will love money, be prideful, and refuse to forgive others—even their family and close friends. They'll slander others to hide their own faults and failures.

Kids, like adults, will be conceited, rash, pleasure-driven, caring more about self-gratification than God and their parents. They'll pretend to be kind and thoughtful, but deep within, all they'll care about is themselves.

So is there any hope? Absolutely! What can you do? Start actively listening to your children. Lead your sons and daughters by example, in both your words and actions. Guide them in the truth. Don't be a dictator. The Bible declares that the truth will set them free. Free from what? All the deceptions Satan is using in an attempt to fill their hearts and minds with fear and confusion. Salvation and direction here on earth and eternal life in heaven—that's what true freedom in Christ is all about.

Really love your kids. Don't yell at them when they aren't saying or doing things exactly the way you want them to. Spend time with them. You don't know which moment with them

---

1   National Campaign to Prevent Teen and Unplanned Pregnancy; also Guttmacher Institute.

may be your last. (Remember, I know.) There is so much more I want to say about our relationships with our children—especially our daughters—but for now, ponder what I've said.

Husbands and Their Wives

We often have our mouth full of boot because of another relationship as well: the one with our wives. I've worked hard providing for my family for over thirty years. I'm sure many of you can relate. Twelve-hour days, six, sometimes seven days a week doing everything I can to keep the roof over their heads, food in their bellies, and clothes on their backs. Surely my wife appreciates and understands all I'm doing for her, right? She's sure to realize I'm doing this for her and the kids. Certainly she can understand why I come home tired and grumpy after a long, hard day's work.

"Hey, honey, this dinner isn't very good."

"Why can't you look as pretty as Jackie?"

"Why are you spending all my hard-earned money?"

"Do the kids really need that?"

"By the way, the guys and I are going hunting this week, but I'll take you out to dinner at the best place in town when I get home to show you just how much you mean to me."

"What, dear? It's your birthday? Really! I made plans with my buds to go fishing tonight. Can't you just go out without me? Of course, I really love you. What does that have to do with me going fishing on your birthday?"

"Wow! That dress looks great on you. It cost *how much*? On second thought, it doesn't look that great."

Open mouth, insert boot.

Men, if we're not careful, we'll find ourselves in 2 Timothy 3. Without the Lord's help, we will not be able to have a truly godly, mutually beneficial relationship with our wife. Remember, Jesus says very clearly the words coming from our mouths are from our hearts.

And just one more piece of advice on how you should treat your wife: Don't ever compare her with your mother, sister, aunt, or any other woman. If you do, be prepared to run to the bomb shelter.

Watch Your Mouth!

We must also watch how we act and what we say around others. We can make lifelong friends or forever enemies with the words we speak. Regardless of our intentions, even if we're joking, the things that come from our lips will impact those around us.

"Dang, Joe, you're a heck of a good worker. Too bad you don't ever show up."

"Hey, Bill, you're really a good boss—when you're not here!"

Even if both statements were true, we exemplified godlessness instead of godliness. We did nothing to encourage "Joe" and "Bill."

"Therefore, there is now no condemnation for those who are in Christ Jesus" (Romans 8:1).

We pick *on* people and pick *at* them, but seldom do we pick *up* people. Sure, we'll say a kind word here and there, maybe while gritting our teeth, but lifting up a brother when he's down is anything but the norm in our society. For every kind word, we offer two critical ones. Thousands of years later, we're still dealing with the same issues Job did with his so-called friends.

More recently, when Jesus walked the earth, it was still

common practice to open mouth and insert—in their case—a sandal. As a people, the Jews despised the Samaritans. They would walk miles out of their way to avoid encountering these neighbors.

And women? Well, let me tell you how they felt about the fairer sex. Jesus was considered a rabbi—a teacher—as were the Pharisees. As "spiritual leaders," the Pharisees would pray each morning before rising. Sounds impressive, huh? Not so much. Their poor wives would have to listen as their dear husbands included in their prayer, "Thank you, Lord, for not making me a woman." Here they were putting their feet in their mouths and they weren't even out of bed yet.

Just think how they felt about a *Samaritan woman.* Seriously!

You can get the picture by reading about the disciples returning to the well where they'd left Jesus. They found Him speaking with a local villager. Yes, you guessed it; it was a Samaritan woman. To make matters more confusing, she was drawing water in the middle of the day. This has led some to speculate that she was a woman of ill repute. Why wouldn't she be there in the early morning before the scorching sun was high overhead?

The disciples were confused. Why on earth was their Master, a Jewish rabbi, speaking with this woman? Surely He knew the proper protocols. One just didn't spit in the face of tradition. At least they knew enough to hold their tongues. In this case, they avoided the foot in mouth issue.

They weren't the only ones who were confused. The Samaritan woman herself asked Jesus why He was speaking to her. From the scriptural account, it doesn't seem that it took too long for her to clue in. When she realized who He was, she ran back to her village. She urged all who would listen to come and see the man who knew all about her—even before she told Him anything. This despised Samaritan woman became an evangelist, leading others to the Savior.

With God's help, we can learn to speak words of love, kindness, and caring.

"I know you had a long day. Thank you so much for preparing dinner." Now there's a comment that just might get you an extra good kiss.

"Dear daughter, that may not be my favorite outfit, but hey, what does Dad know about fashion?" While we want to encourage our daughters to dress modestly—that's another topic altogether—just because we don't like something doesn't mean we should always express our opinion.

And wouldn't it be much better if we encouraged our sons by saying, "So you missed the ball; there's always next time"?

Don't end up with a mouthful of leather as I have so often. Just ask my wife.

In Summary

- It's easy to end up with a mouth full of boot. Perhaps we're not thinking. Perhaps we're trying to impress our buddies. Perhaps we're don't realize "the tongue has the power of life and death, and those who love it will eat its fruit" (Proverbs 18:21).

- We can build up or tear down with even the simplest comment. We must intentionally seek to build up others.

- It is especially important to build up our sons and

daughters. The people they become has a lot to do with how we treat them and what we say to them.

- Our wives need us to pour into their lives. They need our love and support to flourish and become all they can be.

- Whether speaking to a family member, a co-worker, or a stranger on the street, it's vital that we choose our words carefully. When we do, we can share the truth and change lives for the better.

Consider this . . .

1. So how well do you communicate with your kids? Do you do all the talking? Yell? Ignore them? Put them down—or build them up? This week, be more aware of your conversation patterns. Write down your observations. What are you doing right? How could you improve? Determine to become a listener—and to insert boot much less often. Determine to use your words to build them up and guide them—not put them down and discourage them.

2. And how about your wife? Think of at least three times recently you have been insensitive and filled your mouth with boot. What are you going to do about it? What active steps will you take to do better?

3. Think about conversations you've had with others this week. Are there any that would embarrass you for Jesus to hear? (Guess what—He was there!) Ask Him to help you do better.

Chapter 5

Worn Out Blue Jeans

FAMILIES USED TO EAT SUPPER TOGETHER. NO CELL PHONES. No TV. No iPods. They would tell each other about their day and enjoy a home-cooked meal. "God is great; God is good; let us thank Him for our food" was a familiar prayer. The prayer, like the tradition of family meals, is all but extinct.

However, when I was growing up, they were both commonplace. My mother taught me this simple prayer when I was a preschooler. She said, "Now, Roger, let's fold our hands, bow our head, and close our eyes." What a simple childlike prayer! But if you ponder the words for a moment, you'll find they are extremely powerful.

God is good and wants nothing but good for us. He watches over us like a mother watches over her children. In addition, God is great. He asked Job, "Who put the stars in the sky and who made the seas and the mountains?" God asked if Job was there when He created life. Job realized he was small and God was big. Well, duh!

We should remember to thank God for the food He

provides. If He weren't good, if He weren't great, He could let us starve. Most of us believe we provide for our families and, by God's grace, He allows us to do just that. However, without His ongoing gifts of strength, health, and breath, we couldn't get up in the morning, go to work, and earn the money that provides for the needs of our families. We don't like to admit it, but we really are dependent.

The Challenge

Guys have a tendency to hide their emotions more than women. We don't generally talk about our problems. A man will carry around hurt, pain, failure, and loss of direction his entire life. Men will let pride destroy their relationships with their families, cause them to lose a perfectly good job, and even land them in divorce court over something silly. We bull riders have a tough time talking to other bull riders. We also have a challenging time talking to the One we should talk to first and often, not last or seldom, our Lord and Savior Jesus Christ.

I don't have this talking to God thing nailed down, but I do pray . . . when driving my car . . . when walking in the park . . . even when I'm shopping. I don't pray at a specific time. It can be anywhere at anytime—early in the morning, late at night, whenever. Dressed in a suit, my shower towel, or worn out blue jeans—makes no difference. Sometimes my prayers are short and simple. Other times, my conversation is endless. No matter what, I'm sure God hears me. I also know, like most everyone, I don't talk to Jesus often enough.

Don't know how to pray? Afraid of what others may think or say if they heard you? Too much sin in your life to talk to the Master? Not true. He wants to hear from you, guaranteed.

I want to challenge you to pray, and pray often, even if

you find it rough and unnatural at first. Prayer is the open line of communication between you and the Great I Am. Talking to God is not nearly as hard as some make it out to be.

Communicating with the Almighty isn't about going through the motions—it is about learning to carry on a real conversation with Him. Your words should be your own, not someone else's. He's not interested in hearing from just famous people. He wants to hear from you, just a regular working Joe. So be honest with Him, even when what you have to say is embarrassing, shameful, or downright ugly.

Cry out from your heart. Don't be afraid to call out to God. You may speak softly at times and other times not at all. Just speak as you normally do. Be mindful that you are speaking to God, so do it with humility and reverence. Pray—for others first and then for yourself.

Getting Started

We may not be used to praising others or saying thanks, but our Provider in heaven deserves our praises and expressions of thanksgiving. Who else can take the good, the bad, and the ugly and accomplish something awesome? It's all part of His master plan. We really should spend time thanking God for what He's done for us. If you think about it, He's done a lot.

That alcoholic brother-in-law . . . your aging parents . . . your shaky marriage . . . your wayward child . . . your overworked church leaders: God wants to hear you appeal for them all.

And just how should you pray for yourself? Ask God to bless the work of your hands. Ask for the wisdom and knowledge you need. Want to make a difference in a dark world? Ask Him to shine His light in and through you. And that darkness from within—the lust, weakness, fear, and doubt—pray about that too. Problems with money? Your boss? Your family? Get real with God.

We can pray when we're on the run, but there comes a time when we have to put on the brakes and just stop. Too much craziness and too much noise and we might not hear what He has to say. Job and his friends had to zip their lips to hear the Almighty speak, and we do too. We can't just lay out our plans and ask God to endorse them. His plans are far better and far bigger than ours, and we best listen.

Take a deep breath, step back from the insanity of your life, and let the Big Boss speak. Often God infiltrates our mind with His Word. Other times, He lays a heavy burden on our hearts. If we listen closely, we'll find the Holy Spirit prompting us to go to a verse or a chapter in the Bible where He has already laid out the answer. We simply have to read and obey.

One thing is for sure: "Faith by itself, if it is not accompanied by action, is dead" (James 2:17). You can't just hope God will do something great in your life; you have to talk to Him about it and then be willing to put forth some effort. Don't buy into that "bless me all the time" game. God doesn't just throw out free blessings simply because we think He should.

I don't know what Bible so many people are reading these days, but the God I read about in my Bible is a righteous God, a fair God, and a God who watches over His kids. Look in the book of Psalms, the book of Proverbs, or any of the other sixty-six books that make up the Scriptures, and you'll see who God blesses and why. He's not about to play Santa Claus. He's not a fairy godmother or the Easter Bunny. He is the one and only true King.

We can't come running to God only when we need Him to bail us out of our troubles. We can't just call Him God on

Sunday and then live our lives without so much as thinking about Him for the rest of the week.

If our blue jeans aren't worn out, maybe it's time to start spending more time on our knees. Don't have the time? Let me ask you this: If you don't have time to talk to the One who has all the answers, what do you have time for?

Me, Me, Me

"God, I'm sick. I gorge on junk food and shovel down the ice cream like someone's gonna steal it. Yeah, I know I'm fat, but would you please heal my body?" (Are you kidding me?) "I got fired from my job a couple years back and I haven't been able to find work since. Sure, I didn't show up to work on time. I wasn't the only one. I may not have done my best, but it was such a lousy job . . . I'd really appreciate it if you'd find me something else, maybe something in upper management. Yeah, I'd do really well there. And by the way, I lost my car about the same time I lost my job, so I could really use another one. Next year's model would be nice."

I wonder if God shakes His head and rolls His eyes and says, "Oh sure, man, I've got you covered. Let me see now . . . You overeat. You admit you're lazy. Bottom line, you want something for nothing and now, you're calling on me to see what I'm going to do to fix things. That about right? Well, first I'd like you to do a few things for me while I work on answering your prayer."

"Sure, God, whatever you say. Just bless me."

"Listen up! I'm about to speak." (Remember Job?) "Put away those credit cards you're living on. They're giving me a bad name. Debt is not a good thing. Second, I want you to walk to the nearest store or factory and ask for any job they have open. Third, I want you to take your first paycheck and buy some tennis shoes. Every day . . . yes, *every day* . . . I want you to walk just as fast and as long as your body will let you. I mean really push yourself, not just for five or ten minutes. I'll even let you walk on Sundays.

"Since you lack basic wisdom and knowledge about how I want you to live, it's time to start studying the Bible. Open the Word to the book of Proverbs and read a while. Then spend some time in the gospel of Matthew. Wrap up your time by spending a few more minutes reading Ephesians. I speak through my Word and I have lots to say to you."

"Um, Lord . . . This is your child. Remember? I'm sick. No job. No money. Maybe if you'd just send the winning lottery ticket my way . . . If you let me win the jackpot, I can do what you want. And that list . . . I'm not even sure it's really you speaking to me. Maybe it's the devil putting these thoughts in my head. After all, God loves me. He would never make me do all that."

Has this ever been your thinking? Praying in faith doesn't mean expecting God to hand over everything on a silver platter. You can be sure He expects you to work hard. He answers prayer but not always when and how we think He should.

God's Economy

The prayers of a righteous man accomplish much. And just who is this righteous man? Someone who never sins? No. If that were true, none of us qualify. God's definition of a righteous man is one who has been "made right" with Him through a relationship with Jesus Christ, His Son. As we spend time working on our relationships, they get stronger and we mature. The same is true of our walk with God. He enables us to live a more holy and righteous life.

Don't get me wrong about holiness and righteousness. I'm a father, small business owner, and chief bottle washer. I'm a failure at times and down on my knees at others. I'm a working man striving to serve my Lord and living as a follower of Jesus Christ all the days of my life. I have a daughter—and my heavenly Father—in heaven I want to spend eternity with. The pits of hell afford me nothing I'm interested in. I don't want my GPS to lead me down the wrong road. I'm heaven-bound, and I hope you are too.

How do I know God hears prayer? When my wife and I first married, I was working at a job that barely paid our rent, $203 a month plus other living expenses. I asked my boss for a raise but was turned down. He said the company couldn't afford to pay me more at the time. I had given some thought to venturing out on my own but really didn't have the experience or the financial resources to do so. However, once turned down for the measly fifty-cent an hour raise, I realized I had gone as far as I could with that company and had nothing to lose by trying something different.

I started my little company with some help from my dad and my father–in–law, who was a laid off truck driver at the time. I had about $2,500 in total assets. My wife worked in the baby unit at one of the local hospitals. Although her pay was helpful, it just wasn't enough to meet our monthly obligations. I worked every odd job I could find that first year in business. Some nights I was stacking fish on trucks, others shoveling snow. I also split and sold firewood, sanded vehicles, delivered holiday baskets, and on and on. You name it and I did it, anything and everything I could to make a buck.

When I incorporated my company, I prayed a simple

prayer: "God, you see our needs. I don't need to get rich or anything. Just please allow me enough work to pay our bills and make a living." That was it, nothing outrageous or elaborate. Just simple, honest, and to the point.

As I said, we had about $2,500 to our name. In 1983, at the end of the first year in business, I sat looking at the checkbook. I thought my wife had made a mistake, but she told me there was no mistake and the balance was correct. I begin to weep, realizing God had answered my prayer. We had over $13,000 in our account. Equally amazing, we had taken a vacation and had given away some money to a struggling young couple worse off than us. The Lord answered my prayer. He saw my faith in Him, watched as I added work to my faith, and He blessed me with His favor.

Answered Prayer

Was it always easy? Absolutely not! God answered my prayers another time when our daughter was seventeen. Satan used a young boy to deceive her, and she ran away from home with him to get married. The morning she left, we called the local police, the state police, our friends, family, and a man we knew who had a private investigating business. They all said pretty much the same thing: "She's seventeen. They've been gone for a while now. If she doesn't want you to, I highly doubt you'll find her. She'll call you when she's ready."

My wife and I cried and pleaded with God. "Candace has health problems, God. This boy is deceiving her. She doesn't know what she's doing. Help us. We need you."

We yelled when we prayed. It hurt so badly I thought both my wife and I were having heart attacks. Then while we were standing in our kitchen, the Spirit of God did something in me I can't remember ever happening before. I saw a vision of where Candace was. I could see her and the boy she was with sleeping in his car. They were at a rest stop in southern Ohio. (We were in Michigan.)

By faith, my wife and I jumped into one car and two of our friends jumped into another. We started speeding down the highway, working our way to southern Ohio. Unbelievably, after stopping at a few other rest stops, my wife and I pulled into yet another—and guess what we found. Our daughter and this boy were sound asleep just about seventy-five miles north of the Kentucky border. Just as God said, they were still in Ohio.

Candace's life was full of adventure: some good, some bad. My point is this: The Lord answered our prayers! When everyone said it was hopeless, He said, "Roger, I'm still the Great I Am and I hear your prayers." Only God, by His Spirit, could allow my mind to picture exactly where our daughter was. Only God, who loves His children, can do what no other god or human can.

If you still doubt that prayer is vital, consider Jesus. If our Savior, our Redeemer, took time to get away and converse with His Father—even after exhausting days of traveling, healing, and teaching—we should follow His example and do the same.

So how about you? Are your jeans worn in the knees? Do you pray often or barely at all? Are you too busy tweeting, chatting, making the God of all space—not just MySpace—wait to hear from you? The Lord loves to hear from you. He wants to have conversations with you. In fact, He'd like to talk to you on a regular basis.

Not convinced that prayer works? Think again. Check out the story of Moses. See how many times God listened and answered his prayers. What about Paul the apostle or Peter the fisherman, who, by the power of God, healed many? Even Jesus Himself, being both man and God, prayed often to His Father. If Jesus knew the importance of communicating with the Almighty, then we should too.

Did you ask Him what job you should take? . . . Who you should marry? . . . Where you should live? Did you talk to Him before you bought that last car? . . . Took that last vacation? . . . Watched that last movie?

How about this? Go out and buy a brand new pair of blue jeans and see if you can wear out the knees sooner than later. Talk to our Eternal Father . . . it just may be the best investment you'll ever make.

In Summary

- There is truth in the old prayer "God is great. God is good. Let us thank Him for our food . . ." He provides for us and wants us to remember to thank Him.

- We don't have to perfect our technique before making prayer a regular part of our lives. There is always more to learn.

- It's all well and good to bring our wants and needs before the Lord, but it's also important to pray for others. When we do pray for ourselves, we must remember we have personal responsibilities. "For even when we were with you, we gave you this rule: 'The one who is unwilling to work shall not eat'" (2 Thessalonians 3:10).

- Every believer should wear out the knees of countless pairs of blue jeans.

Consider this . . .

1. Name your blessings. Take the next seven days to build a list of what God has done—and is doing—for you. Write the blessings on paper, make a list on your smart phone, or tablet. Whatever works for you. And then start thanking God for those blessings. Let this begin a lifelong habit!

2. What is one of your biggest challenges right now? Are you trying to meet that challenge in your own strength? Get down on your knees—today—and begin asking God to help you.

3. As you continue to build your communication skills with your kids, wife, and others . . . begin to listen for needs you can pray about. Let them know you will be praying. If you don't already have one, start a list of these needs—and as the answers come, add them to your praise list! (Remember, the answers may not come the way or time you planned—but they will come.)

4. This week, share a need you have with at least one other person and ask for prayer.

Chapter 6

Bulldozer

MOST GUYS GET A KICK OUT OF ANYTHING BIG: SKYSCRAPERS, huge sports stadiums, and massive machinery. And speaking of machines . . .

For sheer, raw power, I can think of nothing better than a Cat D-9 or D-10 bulldozer. Talk about flexing your muscles! Those dozer blades can push tremendous amounts of earth, filling and leveling to precision. These machines can also multitask with the best of them, perhaps making the bulldozer the backbone of modern heavy-duty construction.

Imagine we're watching a road crew. The Interstate is being widened to eight lanes and a new cloverleaf is being constructed. Over to the left is a D-10 smoothing fill to even out the roadbed. Another is loosening the packed earth where the old cement lanes used to be. Here comes my personal favorite: a D-9 pushing a full belly-dump with its blade. The dump lacks the power to get up and go with a full load. But the dozer? Piece of cake! Imagine the power it takes to move that huge earthmover *and* its load! Impressive!

Dozers don't zip around the construction site like a four-legged deer, but it's unfair to call them plodders. They are heavy-duty, steady workers. They're slow but sure. They move it, push it, pull it, bury it, and loosen it.

Despite how easy it looks, operating one of these brutes is complicated. Get a fraction of an inch off and your building will lean, your overpass won't meet, and your field won't drain. Great engineering and all those fine-tuned plans will be down the tubes. All it takes is to tilt that big blade just a hair too far up or down, left or right, and you have a disaster.

Working with this equipment takes patience—and tons of it. A freeway may take years to complete. Back and forth. Back and forth. Blade up. Blade down. Carve out a strip. Push it over there. Level it out. Pack it down. Day after day, the operator guides the behemoth until all the grades are perfect.

Precision is just as important as patience. Guiding one of these muscle machines to do precision work requires the touch of a skilled craftsman. One hand controls the blade; the other steers. Repeated adjustments are made to do a perfect job.

Now look at it from the other side of the coin. Maybe you're the best of the best operators. However, if the engineering plans are off or the foreman gives the wrong instructions, you'll still end up in trouble. A solid master plan combined with ongoing supervision is vital if the operator is to succeed.

What a great comparison to the life of a servant of Jesus! He is dependable, able to do important, though often not glamorous, jobs. He is faithful. Turn the switch, pull the starter, shift 'er into gear—and off the dozer rumbles. We too must steadily move from one task to another until each project is wrapped up. Then it's up onto the proverbial trailer we go and away to the next job.

The driver of this mega machine is in charge. We too have a driver, a boss. God is His name, the Almighty. The same has been true throughout history. Look at the life of Joshua. He learned from one of the most well-known leaders in Christian history: Moses. God chose Moses because He knew this guy was up for the task, a very big project. Even so, Moses was like the rest of us. He blew it from time to time. In fact, God would not allow him to enter the Promised Land. Enter . . . Joshua. He would have to follow the instructions of the Divine Operator through some pretty hilly territory.

Uneven Terrain

The terrain we face can be rugged too. That irritating co-worker. That unreasonable boss. That friend who leaves us hanging time and time again. And how about those mountains of sickness, poverty, dependency . . . death? Trying to overcome these obstacles without the right equipment is like trying to dig the hole for a skyscraper's foundation with a teaspoon. It may be slow going at times, but pushing dirt with a bulldozer is far more effective than using a hand shovel. We need the right equipment and the right operator to level the terrain of our lives.

That terrain is often hilly to say the least. We dash off to work and our wives are in and out. Take the kids to school. Pick them up. Doctors. Dentists. Orthodontists. Soccer. Baseball. Volleyball. Church on Sunday. Prayer meeting with the guys every Friday morning. Hunting. Fishing. Bills to pay. Whew! Let's face it, men: Life can be a blur.

Able to multitask or not, a bulldozer operator doesn't try to do everything at once. He moves and works with direction and purpose, making every effort to do the job right the first time. Slow and steady gets the job done. Even though there may be much to do, the work is always done in order of priority. Things that need to be done first get done first.

Our Creator says, "Be still and know that I am God" (Psalm 46:10). We need to slow down at times and make room for the important things. Spend time talking to Jesus and reading His Word. Invest time in your children's lives. They need more than a chauffeur; they need you. Drag out the vacuum and buzz over the floors once in a while. That's a great way to show your wife you love her.

"Yeah, right! Even if I do all that, my problems are still going to be here," you might say.

Maybe they will and maybe they won't. Chances are pretty good they won't disappear overnight. But as your attitude toward God and your family improves, so will your mind-set regarding your circumstances. As your faith grows and you believe what God says, you'll find peace and joy even amid life's storms.

Two thousand years ago, Jesus calmed the storm. He still does. Not only that, He's the project designer, engineer, and supervisor all rolled into one. He wants to ride with you to guide every flick of the joystick, every thought. You see, none of us have the infinite patience and precision to tackle the mountains of life, but Jesus does. And thankfully, He's made that offer to us struggling bulldozer operators.

In It for the Long Haul

Let's take a look at our man Joshua. This dude was an A-1 dozer operator if ever there was one.

Joshua started life in perseverance mode. He was one of the children of Israel who grew up a slave in Egypt. When God, through Moses, called His people out of bondage and led them through the parted waters of the Red Sea, Joshua was in the crowd. He learned patience to a degree we can't even fathom. I mean some of us get impatient waiting for our two-minute coffeepots to brew us a cup. A red light? Sheer agony!

But Joshua gives us a great example of the bulldozer way of life. According to some scholars, the Hebrews made it to the border of Canaan, the Promised Land, in about a year. Twelve guys were chosen for a recon mission. *Just what is God getting us into?* Though the enemy could strike fear into the hearts of even the bravest of men, Joshua knew they had nothing on the Almighty. These dudes were huge, numerous, and plentiful, but Joshua was confident if God said the Hebrews could take them, then they could. However, only one other spy agreed with him. Because of the rampant lack of faith, God led His people into the desert, where Joshua would endure years of wandering around with his fellow Israelites. Talk about perseverance!

And when the time came—four long decades after he was ready to go for it—Joshua led them in with courage and faithfulness. The first obstacle in their journey: the city of Jericho. It had to be leveled. But how? The walls were massive and apparently impenetrable. What does this mighty warrior do? He leads them on a hike. Around the city they go, once a day until the seventh day. Then, it's seven times around. The trumpets. The war cry. The collapsing walls. The commander of the army got his marching orders from the Ultimate Commander in Chief. And victory was theirs.

Joshua led the Israelite army time and again as God had instructed him, driving out the inhabitants of the land. Near the end of his life, when some had begun to worship the false gods of the Canaanites, Joshua gathered the people and said, "Choose for yourselves this day whom you will serve . . . as for me and my household, we will serve the Lord" (Joshua 24:15). You and I must choose also.

Now the bulldozer life is no picnic. Just ask Joshua! Dozers may be powerful machines, but they need regular maintenance. Guys, be sure to get quiet time away from the rat race. Plug into some quality talks with your eternal Boss, and you'll be amazed how quickly the loads of life lift from your shoulders—even if the circumstances don't change right away.

Consider Your Building Project

Take a look at those closest to you—your wife, your children, and your friends. God gave them to you to share your life. Their lives are more valuable than the most lucrative construction site. The Lord God is molding and shaping their lives—and you play a big part in the outcome. It will take patience and perseverance. Sometimes you'll have to walk alongside them and let them set the pace. Other times you'll have to challenge them to choose to walk in God's way.

The crew that comes behind the bulldozer won't have anything to work with unless the machine has done a good job, has followed the plan. You have to do the same. Get on your knees and ask for help. Pore over the instruction manual (aka the Bible). Get a clear picture of the final project and your role in bringing it to be. Then shift down, set your blade, and dig in. Your kids deserve a father who is a man after God's heart. Your wife deserves a man who will love her and give godly leadership. Your friends need a true friend, not one like Job's.

And beyond the walls of our homes are others who need us to help them become leaders following Jesus' example. "Who, being in very nature God, did not consider equality with God something to be used to his own advantage; rather, he made himself nothing by taking the very nature of a servant, being made in human likeness. And being found in appearance as a man, he humbled himself by becoming obedient to death—even death on a cross!" (Philippians 2:6–8).

Sure it costs a lot of money, time, and effort to strengthen the saints and spread the gospel. But way back at Calvary, Jesus Christ, God in human flesh, gave His life so you and I—and everybody who believes in Him—can have a real life now and live forevermore with Him. All the development projects in the world added together cost nothing compared with what our forgiveness and doorway to abundant life cost our Father. And He willingly paid the price for you and me.

Jesus must be at the controls. Life is a long-term thing. Only He knows how you fit into His master plan day by day. He can mold and shape the contours of your life until it becomes useful. Only He can see the soft spots and rocks just below the surface, the dangers that can ruin a foundation. Only He can tell where the floodwaters may run and a ditch needs to be dug.

In the end, what separated Joshua from his countrymen was his focus. Every operator who works for God's construction company, even though he concentrates on the task at hand, always has an eye on the outcome: what that bridge or building will look like someday. Joshua always kept a godly view of the Promised Land in his mind's eye. And that's what we modern-day Joshuas must do too. We have to keep our eye on our final goal: heaven and eternity with Jesus. "Do not throw away your confidence; it will be richly rewarded. You need to persevere so that when you have done the will of God, you will receive what he has promised" (Hebrews 10:35–36).

Yeah, there's a mighty big job ahead. Roll up your sleeves. Hop on board. Lower the blade. And dig in. With Jesus at the controls, even the most challenging project in your life can be accomplished.

In Summary

- Bulldozers do the heavy work, but they do so slowly and with purpose. The things in our lives worth doing will take a lot of patience and hard work.

- Without a reliable plan to follow, even the most diligent bulldozer operator cannot accomplish the task at hand. We need God's Word to give us direction and to accomplish the plans and purposes He has for our lives.

- We are sure to encounter hilly terrain in the course of our lives. But with the right instruction (the Bible) and the right operator (God), we'll make it.

- Just like Joshua on the border of the Promised Land, we may be ready to move forward. However, sometimes those around us aren't. With love and patience, we must walk with them and be willing to give leadership when God opens the doors—even though it may take years.

- From your study of God's Word and from His work in your heart and mind, decide what kind of life you want to provide for your family. Decide how you're going to get there and what steps you have to take to make it happen. Then let down the blade, and may the work begin.

Consider this . . .

1. Think about the terrain each of your children is facing right now. Pray for wisdom in knowing how to help them.

2. Consider the terrain your wife is facing. Are there pits and bumps you can help her with? How can you encourage her to trust God through them? Pray for wisdom. Pray for her.

3. Prayerfully examine your priorities. Chances are God will show you some adjustments that need to be made. Through prayer and studying His Word, plan specific ways to make those changes. And then do it!

Chapter 7

Jesus Loves The Working Man

Up from the Well

FAVORED SON. PROPHETIC DREAMER. FUTURE STATESMAN. SOUNDS pretty good, doesn't it?

However . . . it was no cakewalk for Joseph.

Because of his bold speaking and lack of tact, this young man got himself into a heap of trouble. He was already Daddy's favorite, so his brothers weren't particularly fond of him. When he said God had revealed they would bow down to him, they were royally ticked. And who wouldn't be?

"Go check on your brothers," dear old dad instructed one day. And off went Joseph, totally oblivious to what was about to happen.

When they saw him in the distance, his brothers hatched a plot. Before he knew it, Joseph was stripped of his designer coat and tossed into a dried up well.

"Hey, what gives?"

Their hearts were murderous, but God had other ideas. A

caravan appeared on the horizon and Joseph's brothers came up with a new plan.

"Why go to the trouble of killing this troublemaker? We'll sell him into slavery, tell Pops a wild animal got to him, and then we'll be done with it. So much for his plans to rule over us!"

Insert tented, drumming fingers and sinister laugh here.

Life may not have looked like Joseph expected, but God's favor never left him. He ended up in the home of one of Pharaoh's officials. Everything he put his hands to prospered. His master trusted him implicitly, but there was the little matter of the lady of the house. Well, she wasn't a lady exactly. She very much wanted Joseph to sleep with her, and when he wouldn't, she was furious.

It was likely with a catch in her throat that she told her husband, "That . . . that Hebrew tried to force himself on me. When I called for help, he got out of here so fast he left his cloak behind. See?"

Potiphar was infuriated. He had Joseph tossed into prison post haste. Even there, however, God was with this young man.

The guards entrusted him with responsibilities, and they weren't disappointed. Among other things, God gave Joseph an understanding of dreams. Two of his fellow inmates found out about it and came to him for answers. He informed them one would be killed and the other reinstated into Pharaoh's service. And that's exactly what happened.

Joseph had only one request. "Remember me when you get your job back." But it didn't happen—not right away, at least.

One day Pharaoh had a dream of his own. Even his wisest advisors were clueless about what it could mean. Then it dawned on the cupbearer. "Oh, yeah! I know someone who can help, most powerful Pharaoh."

They called for Joseph. From prison to the king's court— quite a change. God gave Joseph the interpretation of the Pharaoh's dream. The Egyptian ruler was so impressed he elevated Joseph to the position of governor.

The famine Pharaoh's dream had warned them about was soon upon them. Because of Joseph's excellent leadership and organizational skills, Egypt was ready. And when the disaster spread to the surrounding lands, there was enough grain stored in Egypt to share—for a price.

The famine affected Governor Joseph's family and soon his brothers were standing before him. Yes, these men who years before had tried to prevent God's plans from coming to pass were now bowing to the same brother they had once planned to kill—but they didn't recognize him. Joseph, on the other hand, knew exactly who they were.

Here was the perfect opportunity to turn the tables on them. In the end, however, this was how God orchestrated the fulfillment of Joseph's prophetic dream. The second youngest of Jacob's sons ended up providing for his entire family. In fact, the whole family picked up and moved to the land of Egypt.

As Joseph said, "What they planned for evil, God used for good."

The Lord Almighty once again proved Himself sovereign. And His chosen instrument of provision and blessing had been a willing "working man."

Darn Traffic

5:30 am: "Honey . . . time to get up."

Our modern day Joe hits the snooze button, rolls over,

and pulls the covers tightly around his body. "Just five more minutes."

6:00 am: "Darn traffic! I'm going to be late—again. Can't any of these people drive?" Joe leans on the horn. "Get out of the way!"

6:33 am: "You were supposed to be in your truck and rolling three minutes ago. Do we have a problem? You know . . . in this economy, there are lots of people who would love to have your job."

Can you relate? Feel more like a Joe than a Joseph? Ever felt as though you just want to throw up your hands and say, "Why do I even try? I can't please anyone and I can't get ahead. Why bother? Why go to work in the first place?"

And the mind games continue. "No one at work could care less about me. My family doesn't appreciate what I do for them. That Scrooge of a boss hasn't given me a raise in . . . I can't even remember the last time. To top it off, I'm the brunt of one joke after another just because I mentioned I'm a Christian and go to church."

Maybe you've asked yourself one of these questions—maybe all of them. Do you ever feel like throwing in the towel and becoming a couch potato? Are there times when you get so down you find yourself muttering, "Just why am I working anyway? I have nothing to show for it and never have enough money to buy the things *I* want."

So why should you bother?

The Word of God has much to say on the subject.

Take Proverbs 21:25, for instance: "The craving of a sluggard will be the death of him, because his hands refuse to work."

Ecclesiastes 9:10 begins, "Whatever your hand finds to do, do it with all your might."

These are only two of the many passages on the subject.

Let's explore what it means to be a working man from the perspective of the apostle Paul.

The Tent Maker

God promises to bless those who get up every day and give it their best. Want clear direction and rich blessing? God offers both. Paul tells us in 2 Thessalonians if a man is unwilling to work, then he won't eat. Ouch!

Undoubtedly, Paul (formerly Saul of Tarsus) knew what hard work was all about. Before he encountered Christ, he traveled far and wide doing his best to purge the world of Christians. Feared and avoided, he would not be deterred. Trained as a Pharisee, he was determined to do what he thought was God's will—and he thought getting rid of the so called blasphemers was the way to do it. Then one day, he was knocked on his backside by the very God he thought he'd been serving.

After his eye correction, Paul worked harder than ever, sharing the truth about the Messiah. Ask any pastor. Sometimes ministry is anything but glamorous. Dare I say, many North American Christians would throw in the towel if faced with the challenges Paul encountered. He was mocked, ridiculed, imprisoned, shipwrecked, and beaten. And on top of all that, he often had to sweat making tents just so he could eat.

Even so, Paul couldn't help but share the truth. "For when I preach the gospel, I cannot boast, since I am compelled to preach. Woe to me if I do not preach the gospel!" (1 Corinthians 9:16). It was rewarding for the apostle to witness others coming to faith. Many new converts—and older ones as well—were confused about how to apply their Christianity, so Paul helped.

Take the church in Corinth, for instance. Man, did the people there ever need straightening out! Not only did they condone sin, but they also seemed proud of their behavior. And that was only one of their problems. Can you imagine how Paul felt when he heard about what was going on?

"Are you kidding me? They really think that's what it means to be merciful, to be a follower of Christ?"

So the apostle grabbed his stationery and got busy writing. Over the years, he did the same for other churches he'd planted all around the region. He encouraged them. He corrected them. He educated them. Paul became a missionary, a church planter, an author. His was often a thankless—and dangerous—job, but he remained faithful to his work.

I'm certain neither Joseph nor Paul would have chosen the rugged terrain of their lives if it had been up to them. Still, they kept moving forward. Faithful obedience in the face of insurmountable odds is unfamiliar to most. We prefer the quick fix.

Over 72 percent of Americans and millions more around the world say they believe in the God of the Bible. Yet they don't follow His will or His Word. People look at the latest money magazines, the Fortune 500 opinions, and the cable channels often filled with liberal opinions on how to make their money grow. Lottery tickets and get rich quick raffles are always slipping yet another hard-earned dollar out of our pockets. Gimmick after gimmick floats across the screen in front of us, telling us how, with just a small investment, we won't have to work for the rest of our lives. Invest here. Buy there. Soon you'll be living next door to the beautiful people.

Sometimes the last thing we want to do is crawl out of

bed at 5:30 and drag ourselves to what seems like a thankless job. We'd much rather buy into the you-too-can-have-it-all-for-minimal-effort mentality. Feel like a slave to your employer? Here's what the Bible has to say about that: "Slaves, obey your earthly masters in everything; and do it, not only when their eye is on you and to curry their favor, but with sincerity of heart and reverence for the Lord" (Colossians 3:22). Although we are technically not slaves, the same principle applies.

If hard work is important to God, it should be important to us as well.

The Ultimate Worker

And if there's still any doubt, let's look to Jesus Himself as our example. Yes, He was—and is—fully God, but He also became fully human. He grew up among sinful people but never sinned. He had profound wisdom and understanding beyond His years. And yet, He likely worked as a carpenter, following in Joseph's footsteps until he was thirty. Think about that for a moment: The Son of God worked in a skilled trade. It has been speculated that Jesus may have been the primary income earner for a number of years. He was the eldest, and his step-father Joseph isn't mentioned after the incident in Jerusalem when Jesus was twelve. So it is a possibility.

On top of that, Jesus' labor wasn't over when He began public ministry. He walked countless miles. He gathered a ragtag band of society's rejects and taught them about the kingdom of God. Time and again, they looked at Him with blank expressions. Much of what He taught wasn't clear to them until after His death, burial, and resurrection. The crowds pressed in. The religious leaders called Him a child of Satan. The healed often went their way without so much as a thank you.

After a day of trekking cross country, ministering to the hurting, and explaining the secrets of eternity to the disciples, Jesus crawled into a comfortable bed and slept for ten hours. Yeah, right! Often, He found a secluded spot—not easy to do when everyone wants a piece of you—and He prayed. His prayers were more than a recitation of those He wanted God to bless. Remember the sweat "like drops of blood" that poured out in the garden of Gethsemane before His crucifixion? Even His prayer was evidence of great effort.

Let's take a closer look at the last events of Jesus' earthly life.

Jerusalem was overflowing with residents and visitors who had come to celebrate the Passover. Smelly. Noisy. Crowded. Jesus knew He was going to die. In fact, He told His disciples before they made the trip many things that were soon to come, but they still didn't understand. After all, He was the Savior, right? He was going to free them from the tyranny of Roman rule—or so they thought.

Monday can be the most difficult day of the week. We don't want to get out of bed. We don't want to climb into our cars and head to the salt mines—especially if we know it's going to be a particularly difficult week. Imagine how Jesus must have felt. Off he went to Jerusalem, knowing what lay ahead, knowing He would have to face persecution and death *alone*. But He forged ahead with His disciples in tow.

The Messiah was anointed with fine perfume when He was at his friend Simon's house in Bethany. But even that loving gesture was tainted by questions about waste and excess.

When Jesus and His disciples shared the Passover meal, usually a joyous celebration, He was well aware that one of those closest to Him would rat Him out.

When Jesus broke the bread, He knew exactly what it

would represent for eons to come: His very body that would soon be beaten, bruised, and broken for them—for us. When He poured the wine, He saw His own blood pouring from His head, hands, feet, and side.

The custom after the Passover meal was to sing a song. Can you imagine singing, knowing a brutal death was nipping at your heels? After the song, Jesus and His disciples headed to the garden of Gethsemane. It had been an exhausting day, and Jesus' followers couldn't keep their eyes open. While He went off by Himself and pleaded for another way to save mankind, they slept. After He asked them if they couldn't keep watch for a mere sixty minutes, Jesus went off to pray once again. And his companions? In moments, they were again sawing logs.

And then the landscape erupted with activity. Armed troops led by Judas Iscariot appeared on the scene. The disciples were awake now! A brandished sword. A severed ear. A healing touch. Chaos.

They came for Him in force. Jesus could have called legions of angels to come to His defense—but He didn't. He went with them willingly. The Son of God allowed Himself to be found guilty and sentenced to death by men with no legal case or evidence against Him.

After that came the ultimate hard work. Jesus surrendered Himself to one of the cruelest executions ever devised by man. Make no mistake—He could have carried out swift and immediate judgment. Instead, He chose to die for sinners. Yes, the Savior would rise from the dead, but first, He paid the price we never could. Selfless. Hardworking. Overflowing with love for the undeserving. Now that's an example for all of us!

This was why the Son of God came to earth. This was the work He was destined to fulfill. Was it easy? Absolutely not! Did He flinch in the face of the Ultimate Challenge? He did not. Will He give us strength to do the good works prepared in advance for us? (See Ephesians 2:10.) He most certainly will. And why?

Because Jesus loves the working man!

In Summary

- God had amazing plans for Joseph, but the path to those plans included some piercingly dark times. If the light doesn't seem to be shining in our lives, it doesn't mean God has forgotten His promises to us.

- No matter how discouraged and overwhelmed we become at work, the Bible makes it clear we are to be diligent workers—even when we're ready to quit.

- As believers, we are responsible for sharing the gospel and making Jesus known, even if we must do so while continuing our tent-making endeavors (aka our day-to-day work).

- We can learn not only from great men like Joseph and Paul; we can also learn from the Son of God Himself. He could have come to Earth and ruled from some ivory tower, but He didn't. He humbled Himself, rolled up the sleeves of His robe, and worked tirelessly.

- One of the most amazing facts about our Lord is that He knew full well what lay ahead of Him—the lies, the beatings, the crucifixion—yet He worked with His disciples to teach them all they needed to know before He returned to heaven. Whether we have an idea of the battles that are before us or not, with His help, we must be faithful to do what needs to be done here and now.

Consider this . . .

1. "I can't do anything right. It's hopeless. I think even God has forgotten me." Ever feel that way? Describe. What happened? How did you get past that point? Or maybe you are feeling that way now. Time to get your eyes off the circumstances. Time to focus on God. Time to focus on the promises in His Word. Time to run *to* God, not away from Him. Every day this week set aside time to read the Bible and pray. Continue talking to God throughout the day. And then continue that next week . . . and the next . . . and the next. Your circumstances may not change right away—but your attitude will.

2. Had any good pity parties lately? What did they accomplish? Eyes off you! Eyes on God!

3. God has a plan for you. The way may not always be easy. But He loves you and has promised to be with you. Are you willing to work hard each day, trusting Him for the next? Trusting Him for the outcome? I challenge you to begin each day submitting to His plan and determining to give it all you've got.

Chapter 8

Race To Win

"THEY'RE AT THE POST . . . AND THEY'RE OFF!"

Horseracing is such a glamorous sport. Right?

Well, maybe if you're in the stands. But think what it's like on the track. You're perched on a thousand-pound beast that is literally chomping at the bit to break free from the confines of the gate. This animal was born to run. The gate swings open and this half ton of muscle and sinew can't wait to tear up the track. But that's the case with the other horses on the field as well.

Mud. Sweat. Tons of horseflesh all around. Thundering hooves. Every other jockey as intent on winning as you are.

It's all on the line: your pride, your career, your safety . . . and maybe even your life.

The adrenaline is pumping and the possibilities are breathtaking. It takes real work and courage to climb aboard a thoroughbred. Horseracing is definitely not for the faint of heart.

I absolutely love horses. Something about those four-legged beasts has held the hearts of men for centuries. What an inspiration to watch them run as though nothing could hold them back or slow them down!

In 1946, a horse named Assault won three races in five weeks. He won the Kentucky Derby, the Preakness, and the Belmont: the Triple Crown. Twenty-one horses have won two of these three races over the years, but only eleven horses have ever won all three races and earned the Triple Crown Thoroughbred title. With the millions of horses on the planet, fewer than a dozen have been able to win the most prestigious title in the sport of thoroughbred racing.

For Assault, winning was anything but easy. As a one-and-a-half-year-old, he stepped on a surveyor's stake that pushed its way up through his hoof. He was constantly plagued by illness and injury. After one particular race, his owners thought Assault should be used exclusively for breeding. His stamina was lagging. Soon after, they discovered he had a kidney infection.

Assault and his owners faced yet another obstacle. He was born and trained in Texas. Since the first Triple Crown in 1913, all winning horses had come from the great state of Kentucky. In the early 1900s, if your horse wasn't from the Blue Grass State, the odds were nobody would bet on him. However, Assault and his owners had other plans. Although he was supposedly bred in the wrong state and had to deal with illness and injury, against all odds, Assault proved everyone wrong.[2]

---

2   "Assault (horse)." Last updated May 4, 2013. *Wikipedia, http://en.wikipedia. org/wiki/Assault_%28horse%20 (*May 7, 2013).

Our Race

And just what do we have in common with this Triple Crown winner?

> Therefore, since we are surrounded by such a great cloud of witnesses, let us throw off everything that hinders and the sin that so easily entangles. And let us run with perseverance the race marked out for us, fixing our eyes on Jesus, the pioneer and perfecter of faith. For the joy set before him he endured the cross, scorning its shame, and sat down at the right hand of the throne of God. (Hebrews 12:1–2)

Those verses are so rich in meaning. As we examine them, we can clearly see our life as a race.

Assault had to "throw off" obstacle after obstacle on his way to the winners' circle. What obstacles do we have to overcome? What hinders us? There are, of course, external realities we can't change, but there is much we can do. (God wouldn't give us a command He didn't equip us to obey.)

How do we respond to the obstacles that easily entangle us?

"Sundays are my only day to sleep in. Does God really expect me to get up and go to church?"

"Give to the local church? Are you kidding? We're barely making ends meet as it is."

"Hang out with other Christians? They're nothing but a bunch of hypocrites."

"Share the good news about Jesus? I'll just leave that to the preachers and evangelists."

"Love my wife like Christ loved the church? I keep a roof over our heads. Her girlfriends can meet her emotional needs. Plus, she goes to ladies' Bible study. I don't need to read God's Word and pray with her."

"What do you mean I'm responsible for my kids' behavior? I'm too busy earning a living to keep track of what they're doing. I leave that to their mom. Sure she works too, but mothers are better with that kind of stuff."

Recognize any hindrances, any life-choking hurdles?

Yes, the race God set before us includes meeting the physical needs of our families, but even more importantly, it means putting the God of the universe first, getting to know Him, and serving Him by giving leadership in our homes.

So how's your race going these days? Are you in training? Are you in the best shape of your life? Are you preparing to cross the finish line and accept your prize?

I'm sure there were countless days when Assault would gladly have escaped the rigors of training. His owners, however, wouldn't let him. And in the end, the highest honor in horseracing awaited him. The Triple Crown is nothing compared to the prize that lies before the children of the Living God. No matter what dignitary stands poised to place a wreath around the winning thoroughbred's neck, the One who waits for us is so much greater.

In the case of horseracing, that dignitary awarding the prize likely has nothing to do with the horse before that day. Thankfully, that is not the case with "the author and perfecter of our faith." He blazed the trail before us. And now He comes alongside us to show us the right path and strengthen us to run it. Being the God He is, He also stands at the finish line cheering us on, eager to present us with a crown. Wow! Can you imagine?

"Go, Peter, go! Remember, I am the Great I Am, the Only God. I do not fail my children. Go, Peter, go! You can win the race! You can finish big!"

We are to fix our eyes on the One who awaits us, crown in hand. Racehorses wear blinders to keep them from getting distracted, to keep them from getting spooked. We need to wear spiritual blinders. With the hundreds of distractions that cross our paths every day and beckon for our attention, focus is essential. These distractions can certainly be numbered among those things that hinder and entangle us. Morning chaos. Traffic jams. Overbearing bosses. Two-faced co-workers. The office flirt. The kids' extracurricular activities. Video games. TV. Computer recreation. Homework hassles.

While some of these items are hard or even impossible to avoid, to win the race, we must fix our eyes on Jesus. Amid life's busyness, just how do we do this? Make time to read God's Word and pray before starting the day. This will bring order and peace to the chaos. Taking time on the ride to work to talk to God about our family, our job, even those things that divert our attention, can bring calm in the midst of bumper-to-bumper delays. Praying for our boss, co-workers, and those who make inappropriate advances can change us—and them. (Side note: As much as possible, we should avoid those who tempt us to stumble in our walk with God.)

After a crazy day at work, it's tempting to plop on the couch and read the paper, watch TV, or get lost on the Internet. Or we may get so busy running here, there, and everywhere that we lose our focus. What race are you running? The one God has planned? Or your own? We should never confuse running *the* race with simply running non-stop.

Assault didn't win the ultimate honor by running whenever and wherever he wanted. He had to train according to specific standards. And when he was ready, the requirements were precisely laid out. He had to be in the right place at the right time. It wasn't easy, but it was worth it.

Has my personal race been easy? Not a chance. I started at the gate in a small town outside Detroit, Hazel Park. Until I was twenty-one, I lived in this small, hardworking, blue collar community. I remember asking my dad when I was twelve if we could buy a pair of nine-dollar tennis shoes. His response: "Are you out of your mind?" Through my parents' work ethic, God blessed me with a roof over my head, food in my belly, and clothes on my back. However, I did not learn to appreciate all they'd done until much later in life.

Throughout my youth, I was walking with God one day and running away from Him the next. I'd pray, "Oh, Holy Father" on Sunday and raise hell by the time the sun set on Monday. I'd ask God to use my life for His glory, then ask a high school friend if I could share a joint or a shot of whisky. I heard the Word of God preached on Sundays but never took time to read it for myself. I was a Sunday Christian only and I hated it. I detested who I was because I knew who I wanted to be but never had the faith or backbone to get there. As a small boy, I started my race strong, but the older I got, the further back in the pack I wound up. I was losing my eternal race one day at a time.

As a young adult, I went into business. Over the years, I became entangled by all that went with it. The pride. The pressure. The preoccupation. I can relate to this rich young man:

> Just then a man came up to Jesus and asked, "Teacher, what good thing must I do to get eternal life?"

"Why do you ask me about what is good?" Jesus replied. "There is only One who is good. If you want to enter life, keep the commandments." (Matthew 19:16–17)Although the young man felt he'd kept the commandments, he knew there was still a void in his life. He wanted to know what else was required of him. He seemed to be searching for something to make his life worth living, his race worth running. Without the finish line in sight, he was running just to run, and that wasn't cutting it.

Jesus laid it on the line. "If you want to be perfect, go, sell your possessions and give to the poor, and you will have treasure in heaven. Then come, follow me" (Matthew 19:21).

The young man did a 180 and headed the other way. He was not willing to sell all he had, give his profit to the poor, and follow the Messiah. Satan used his pride and reliance on material wealth to lure him away. He does the same to us every chance he gets.

Life is not about the race to the bank or to retirement—and I believe this takes up far too much of our time already. Real life is about the race to eternal life. That's the life that matters to Jesus, and that's the life that should matter to you and me.

The race the Creator set before us isn't erratic and random, although it isn't always clear to us. The Scriptures bring direction and clarity. They reveal whether or not we're actually headed in the right direction. We have to study God's Word, and by the power of His Holy Spirit at work in us, we have to obey it. Our race ends when we cross the finish line and enter heaven. Despite the fact that the nature of God's home and its very existence have been debated for years, according to the Bible, it is a real place.

Even though I've had my fair share of questions about heaven, I know my Savior Jesus is waiting for me there. My goal is to keep my eyes on Him, cross the finish line, and enter glory. I want to live forever with the One who holds my life in His hands. I don't want to be left behind with the pack. I want to break away, cross the finish line, and win the Divine Triple Crown. (Good news . . . in this race, there can be many winners.)

We must run life's race with eternity in mind. We can't allow Satan and the evils of this world to keep us from finishing well. I'm fifty-three years old and wish I could rerun my race—at least forty years of it—but I can't . . . and neither can you. But because of His grace, you and I can get up tomorrow, step into the starting gate, hit the track refreshed, and run the race that is still before us. Don't let the things and the people of this world distract you from running the race of all races. You can be a winner with Christ Jesus.

In Summary

- Horseracing, though apparently glamorous, is a grueling sport—just plain hard work. Though we may not attain the highest prize in our field, day-to-day faithfulness to the task at hand—no matter how challenging—has its rewards.

- Assault, against all odds, refused to listen to the naysayers. With God's help, we too can overcome the obstacles in our path and achieve all He has for us.

- Assault "threw off" the opinion of others, injury, and exhaustion. We too must overthrow the obstacles, within and without, to run the race God sets before us. That race includes hard work, caring for our family, and growing in our relationship with the Lord.

- We have to work hard not only to succeed on the job but also to achieve those things that will cause us to get ahead spiritually: prayer, Bible reading, fellowshipping with other Christians, and more.

- Assault's blinders enabled him to focus on the finish line without distraction. Jesus is "the author and finisher of our faith." We must run with our eyes on Him, focusing only on what He places ahead of us.

Consider this . . .

1. What hurdles are blocking you from becoming all God has designed you to be and doing all He has called you to do? Be real. And be specific. Maybe you have some wrong attitudes. Or your priorities are a mess. Or perhaps there is sin in your life. What are you willing to do to throw off those obstacles? Name some specific actions you will take.

2. How about it? Are you spending a lot of time vegetating? Or maybe you are galloping through life with so much busyness you are missing some of the most important things? Missing what God has called you to do as husband . . . father . . . fisher of men. Ask Him how you can refocus your energies, your diligence, on His plan. Don't just run. Run *the* race.

Chapter 9

Did I Do Something Wrong?

The Walls Are Closing In

Where to begin? It was the fall of 2007. The economy was unstable at best, and by October the stock market decline resembled an avalanche. The financial impact blazed across most of America. My company was right in the thick of this massive crash as many customers cancelled upcoming work. Even larger municipal and commercial clients abruptly put the brakes on projects that represented months of work for us.

I wasn't the only one worried about losing everything. Several of us met together to seek God's direction, peace, and strength. The year 2007 was the start of something that to this day challenges the lives of most men, women, and children. Little did I realize the events that began that year were only the beginning of what would be a series of tests for me . . . and my trust in Jesus Christ.

On October 12, 2008, I was driving home from work when my cell phone rang. "Roger, Bobby is dead."

"What?" I yelled. My fifty-seven-year-old brother gone? No way! "What happened?"

"We're not sure yet. We just found him. He is still lying in his recliner with the football game on." It was a Saturday and my brother loved college football.

Oh, the horror of it all as I drove as fast as I could to Bobby's house. There I found him just like they said—cold and lifeless, lying in his chair.

"Why, God?" I yelled. "What happened? How can this be?"

My brother had recently retired from Chrysler and was working with us at our tree service. He enjoyed working with Dad and me and loved the company as though it were his own. He also loved splitting wood and treated each log as if it were a piece of art. Bobby had a wood-burning stove at home.

On that particular Saturday, he'd apparently picked up some wood from the shop, taken it home, stacked it, and then gone inside to catch the game. My sister-in-law was away at a women's retreat but said she felt something in her spirit telling her to check on Bobby. The retreat was over Saturday morning, and when Chris opened the door, there was Bobby, gone from this world and from our lives forever.

In January 2009, my phone rang with more bad news. This time it was one of my aunts who had died. At fifty-nine, she had gone in for a routine heart valve replacement. Everything seemed to go as planned. Yet within seventy-two hours after her surgery, something went wrong and my wonderful, loving, caring aunt was gone.

Economic challenges still stared me square in the face as I daily cried out to God. "God, I have bills to pay, a family to take care of, a staff with issues of their own who need jobs."

I remember praying more than once, "God, where

are you? I need you to show up and show up big. Did I do something wrong, God?"

On top of this, I asked why Bobby had to die. He was only fifty-seven. He was a good-hearted brother. He was just finding a little true joy in life. And what about his wife, daughter, son-in-law, and especially his four grandchildren? They were his happiness.

And what about my Aunt Janet? She wouldn't hurt a fly or say a bad word about anyone. She went to church, loved God, let her light shine, and did everything she could to be a friend to those in need and to love and support her family. So why didn't God let her live and take some mean old cuss? Little did I know then that things were about to get worse as the storm of all storms was headed our way.

On May 19, 2009, my baby girl Candace died aboard a cruise ship touring the Hawaiian Islands. I just knew God was going to perform a healing miracle in her life. He raised Lazarus from the dead. He parted the Red Sea. He turned water into wine and made the blind see. I believed He was going to heal Candace of her heart condition. Why did God let this happen? What was He thinking? This was my little girl. We served Him, called Him Lord, helped others, paid our tithes, and then some. We did whatever He put in front of us to do. Why couldn't He save our baby from death? Why couldn't He at least let me go first so I wouldn't have to lay her body in the ground?

"Why, God?"

After years of hurting, I still often ask God why. You would think I'd get a little extra measure of grace from the Almighty. One would hope God had plans to send me on a nice long vacation, that my work stress would come down a notch, and that He'd protect all my friends and family for a season so I could recover from all the hurts. One would think, right?

The Struggles Continue

Then 2010 and 2011 turned out to be anything but a vacation. Two different legal battles hit our company and me like mortars falling from the sky. The business had barely moved forward when health issues, family problems, and financial woes blasted most of our staff. This chaos was taking its toll on our company's overall performance.

In July 2011, my mother passed away after years of illness, but there was some comfort in this as we knew she had left this life of sickness and was now healthy, living eternally with Jesus.

By November 2012, my wife and I needed a break and hitched a ride on a speeding airplane bound for Grand Cayman Island, the R and R we so needed. I was convinced this getaway would offer the cure for getting us—and the business—back on the right track. Wrong again! On the fifth day of our sunny vacation, we received word that Rhonda's father, Bob, was diagnosed with Stage Four plastic lymphoma. Cancer! As soon as we landed back in Detroit, Michigan, we were on our way to Troy Beaumont Hospital to deal with what would be yet another "Why, God?" issue in our lives.

You'd think God would know we couldn't handle any more drama in our lives. Wrong again! Very early in 2013, we found ourselves dealing with my dad, who'd had a heart attack combined with a strain of flu that almost ended his life. The virus also triggered a new level of dementia.

Can you see it? One dad in one hospital for twelve days, the other in and out of yet another hospital for months? And there we were—my wife, me, my only sister and my wife's only sister—trying to give 24/7 care to our parents. To top it off, we were battling some kind of flu virus ourselves. My sister, Lynette, was down. My sister-in-law, Deanna, was also down.

Plus, they both had their own households and families to care for. My wife, Rhonda, caught a flu bug as well. But Rhonda never stops going, and I mean never.

During January, my company lost out on two big projects we had done for the previous eight years. We didn't do anything wrong. Another company simply bid the work cheaper. They got the work and we got the boot.

Work was slow. Both dads were suffering. Sickness knocked us all down. What else could happen? One day while trying to walk to the bathroom, Bob, my father-in-law, had a fainting spell. He fell right into his hundred-pound wife Wanda. She then fell into a kitchen counter.

My phone rang and my wife said, "I think my mom broke something and needs to be checked out. I'm the only one here. Deanna is home in bed sick and I can't be in two places at the same time. Can you come take Mom to the emergency room?"

After a long night and a couple of days in Troy Beaumont Hospital, Wanda was diagnosed with three broken ribs and two cracks in her pelvic bones. The doctor said it would take about two to three months for her to heal and get back on her feet. My wife is now living with her mom as she needs 24/7 care. (Her dad recently passed away.) My dad also needs round the clock care. When we thought life couldn't throw us anything else, we got the call that Rhonda's aunt, Bob's sister, had died from cancer. "Why, God?"

Faith Tested

The testing of our faith increases our endurance, our skills, and our trust in God. Our Heavenly Father allows things to happen for a reason. I may not ever know all the reasons and I surely don't understand all of God's ways or His thinking. What I do know is this: He has a perfect plan for my life. As Jesus said, "Not my will, but yours be done" (Luke 22:42).

Have you had your share of moments that cause you to question God? If so, you're in great company. Remember our man Job? Think he ever said those words? He was a great boss, a protective father, and one who believed God was Lord over everything. Look at all he went through. Or what about our guy David, future king over all Israel? For years he was on the run from Saul, who tried every way possible to destroy his competition. Remember David was "a man after God's own heart." Why did he commit adultery? Why did he deceive those in his army in a manner that led to the death of thousands of his own men? What about the death of his young son? You can bet time and again David struggled before the Lord, asking why.

And what about Mary and Martha when they expected the Lord Jesus to save their brother's life? "'Lord,' Martha said to Jesus, 'if you had been here, my brother would not have died'" (John 11:21). You can read the whole story in John 11, but pay particular attention to verse four. A messenger had just brought word to Jesus that Lazarus was ill. "When he heard this, Jesus said, 'This sickness will not end in death. No, it is for God's glory so that God's Son may be glorified through it.'" Why do bad things happen to good people? For God's glory!

I don't know why any brother or sister has to die or why parents have to bury their children. I'm not sure why a mother has to fight illness most of her life and the only relief comes by way of the grave. I can't give you a solid, sure-fire reason a man who has never been in the hospital or seriously ill for seventy-six years is told he has stage four cancer.

Solomon says in Ecclesiastes that one man is found rich

and another poor. One has everything go easily in life while another struggles to make it through each day. The reason is this: It's all part of God's plan.

More Powerful than Any Storm

Amazing as it is—at least to me—no matter what we go through, no matter what storm is in our path, our God is greater, stronger, higher than any of them. His Word doesn't say we won't have challenges in our lives. He says He goes through the fire with us. Some of us will have to jump major hurdles and others will just go over small speed bumps, but either way, He is there with us if we let Him.

"Let Him?" Doesn't everyone want God with them all the time? Sure, when things are at their worst, we want—and even expect—God to show up in a big way. We treat Him like Santa Claus or a genie in a bottle.

> The Son is the image of the invisible God, the firstborn over all creation. For in him all things were created: things in heaven and on earth, visible and invisible, whether thrones or powers or rulers or authorities; all things have been created through him and for him. (Colossians 1:15–16)

We can learn so much from Paul's letter to the Colossians. I encourage you to read the entire book. Notice the end of verse sixteen: "All things have been created through him and for him." Such powerful words! God is the only creator of everything good, including you and me. We were and are made for Him, for His glory, for His purpose. You and I were created because God wanted us.

I'm sure this isn't the most polished, the most perfect book you've ever read or will ever read. Still, I hope with all my rough text you get this point if nothing else: God loves you and me so much He offered His Only Son to pay for our sins. God loves you and me with an unconditional and everlasting love. He loves us as a father loves his children. He cares about every mountain we have to climb. He sees every challenge we face. God desires, more than any of us likely realize, to be there, leading, guiding, and taking us through the fires that come our way. God knows when your marriage is busted wide open. He knows when you're lonely and need a friend. Our Lord sees every hurt and every disappointment. Even when we're far away, trapped in our sins, God still extends His mighty, loving, and gracious hand. He will take hold of us if only we will trust Him and call Him our Eternal Father, our God and Maker, our Savior.

Truth be told, in our flesh, we'd rather live outside the Ten Commandments. As Satan tries daily to deceive us, he wants us to live our lives as far away from God as possible. The deceiver throws every curve he can to keep us running our race in the wrong direction, away from God instead of toward Him. Our culture is so blinded by the liar of all liars that we want to blame God when shootings happen, children are killed, a building is bombed, a husband leaves his wife, a thirteen-year-old becomes pregnant, or a son or daughter turns to an ungodly lifestyle. We use the mightiest of all names in vain and don't think twice about it. When we don't get a raise or are laid off, we complain and blame God. Never be fooled; God loves you and me. He wants His best accomplished in our lives. It is Satan who is seeking to destroy us for all eternity.

Why yell at God when problems come? Why turn from Him when things don't go our way? Why blame Him for all our woes and yet, in our most desperate moments, call out to Him? The God of the universe, the one and only true God, loves you and me more than we'll ever be able to comprehend. We need to run to the Master of the Galaxy. We must stretch out our hands and take hold of His. God is big. He's big in power, big in love, extra big in grace. He's big in wisdom and did I already mention big in love? The Lord Jesus desires to walk this journey with us, leading every footstep we take.

So what's the problem? We are.

God must be a part of our daily lives. He cannot be a Sunday God or an only-when-we- need-Him-God. Let me go back to the question, "Why, God?" I wish I could give you a rock solid answer for everything we face, but I can't. Job didn't fully understand the reasons for his woes. David cried out daily for answers to his questions. Even Paul couldn't figure out why he had to deal with thorns in his life. However, these men knew God was the answer to everything in their lives, the only answer.

Put your trust in God for He cares about everything going on in your life. Keep running toward our Lord, the Master of our souls, Jesus Christ, the author and finisher of our faith and our very lives. One day, sooner than we all realize, this life will be over. Either by way of the grave or by the rapture, our lives here on earth will come to an end. Then what? Where will you go? Where will you spend eternity?

In Summary

- Have you had a week, a year, a decade when heartache after heartache came nipping at the heels of the previous one? You are not alone.

- During those times, have you blamed God? Have you wondered what you had done to deserve everything threatening to bury you? Remember Job. He wasn't perfect, but it wasn't his imperfection or sin that brought about the disasters in his life. Despite how things looked, God had a plan and purpose for it all. I'm convinced He has a plan when our lives are upside down—though I don't always know what it is.

- The storms in our life can threaten to suck us under. The pounding torrent blinds us, and there are times we can't catch a glimpse of light. In John 8:12, Jesus told His listeners He is the light of the world. That light is always shining. We can only see beyond the clouds through eyes of faith.

- If we want to see through eyes of faith, God has to be part of our life 24/7. He is not simply a Sunday God. He is not Santa Claus or a genie in a bottle. We must make time and expend energy to really get to know Him. Then we can trust Peter's words of challenge and promise: "Cast all your anxiety on him because he cares for you" (1 Peter 5:7).

Consider this . . .

1. Are you blaming God for something that went wrong in your life? Describe your feelings. Many blame God for bad things—but blaming Him comes from not knowing Him. How well do you know Him? I challenge you to get better acquainted by spending more time in the Bible. Spending more time talking to Him—and listening. Are you willing to do that? Get started today. You may want to begin by

reading the book of Job and the story of Joseph (Genesis 37–50).

2. When things seem to just keep going wrong, we often blame ourselves. *Did I do something wrong? Is God punishing me?* Again, we need to get better acquainted with God. In some cases we did do something wrong and are suffering the natural consequences. But God is loving—and forgiving. Read 1 John 1:9. Confess. He promises to forgive and cleanse. In other cases, the bad things that happen have nothing to do with anything we did. But if we trust Him, He will help us through—and He will even bring good from it. Are you carrying a load of guilt? It's time to unload. Talk to Him. Let Him love you and help you move on.

Chapter 10
Jesus Is The Real Superhero

SUPERHEROES . . . THEY ARE NOTHING NEW. BACK IN 1938, TWO teenaged boys, Jerry Siegel of Cleveland and Joe Shuster of Canada, created a protagonist for their science fiction story. His name: Superman. They sold their character for only $130 to a radio station producer. As the saying goes, "The rest is history."[3]

Jesus Christ, God's one and only Son, was sent to earth to achieve His divine purpose. Joseph welcomed Him and provided for His needs when the Creator of all that exists humbled Himself and came as a human baby. After thirty years of a fairly average existence—based on what the Scriptures do and do not say about those three decades—Jesus began His public ministry. His words and deeds revealed Him as the world's true superhero. The salvation He brought went far beyond anything the 1938 fictional Superman could give. The Messiah, the King, the Savior—capital S—was victorious at

3   "Superman Publication History," *DC Comics.Wikia: http://dc.wikia.com/wiki/ Superman_Publication_History* (May 7, 2013).

every turn. Even in His death, He was not defeated. The Lord Jesus has been in the business of defeating evil for eons.

Long before Siegel and Shuster came up with their fictitious character and long before the Father sent His Son to earth, God was busy giving real people unbelievable power. Thousands of years ago lived a man named Samson, and the Almighty had some pretty incredible plans for this guy's life.

"Don't cut your hair. Yep, you heard me right. Do not cut your hair."

And Samson didn't for years. His hair was a symbol of the supernatural strength the Lord had poured out on His servant. Lions were no match for him. He tore one apart with his bare hands. A thousand enemy Philistines? No problem. "Just give me the jawbone of a donkey." The gates of an enemy city? He hoisted them out of the ground and carried them off. Mocked by his captors? In a final act of strength, Samson pushed over the supporting columns—with nothing more than his bare hands and divine brute force—killing more of the oppressors that day than he had during his lifetime. Now there was a superhero!

"Yeah, so?" you may be asking. "Where are my super powers to deal with life's day-to-day struggles?"

Maybe you don't feel especially powerful, but my dear fellow bull rider, infinite power is available to you.

Let's talk about some other real examples of His power—beyond what He accomplished in and through Samson's life.

He gave Moses the power to part the Red Sea, and the Hebrews passed through on dry land. The water then swept away their enemies. He gave a young future king by the name of David the courage and strength to stand against the Philistine giant and defeat him. He gave the prophets insight and determination to declare truth even in the face of mocking, scorn, and schemes to end their lives.

Angels announced the arrival of God's Son. However, He chose to send shepherds to welcome the baby. These guys were way down the social scale of their day—let me tell you— definitely not the ones you'd choose to visit the newborn King of kings. He gave them the task of spreading the Good News.

When the baby grew up, Jesus shocked the religious bigwigs of the day and hung out with "sinners," tax collectors, fishermen, and the like. Exalt yourself and God will humble you. Humble yourself before Him, and He will lift you up in unbelievable ways—though not always to success as the world defines it.

Even in His death, Christ exemplified a power few understood. After all, He hung on a cross between the worst of the worst. Death by crucifixion was reserved for the vilest criminals. He paid my debt. He paid your debt. And Jesus paid the debt of the thief who that day joined Him in Paradise. That's a superpower. That's the Real Savior.

God's most amazing superpower is the forgiveness of sin. In Old Testament times, the Hebrews had to make a journey to Jerusalem. For some of them, that was a heck of a long way. No airplanes. No trains. No cars. They had to go to the temple with the best of the best from their flocks. The priests, themselves sinners, would offer all these sacrifices to God. Then it was pack up and head home until the same time the following year. Just imagine if we still had to stand in line to offer a sacrifice for the forgiveness of our sins. Thankfully, that's no longer the case.

Superman is nothing more than a fictional character who can't save anyone. Samson, despite his great feats of strength, only "began to save" God's people from their enemies. But

Jesus Christ, the Son of God, is the Real Deal. He lived a sinless life, died in our place, and rose to bring us victory and power to live in the here and now and throughout eternity. His saving power continues to this day. By God's grace, we must simply accept it.

Throughout the years, I've watched as God brought down the insurmountable walls in my life. I have an idea how Joshua felt as he watched Jericho's wall crash to the ground. The Lord has reminded me just how big He is and that He has everything under control. Job was humbled. I have been too. God Almighty has worked in and through this simple working man. Repeatedly, He has guided my mind and hands. Although I have failed Him far too often, He still allows this bull rider to climb on and ride one more time. He supports me with His love and grace. Jesus has loved this working man as long as I've been alive. He has pulled the boots out of my mouth on a regular basis. And although sometimes I'd like to take the easy route, He guides me like a bulldozer, inch by inch, day by day, pushing me toward His goals for my life.

I came to know God's grace, love, and yes, His superpowers in a whole new way when Candace passed away. There is no way I could have handled it in my own strength. I needed to be there for my wife and son, but I could barely hold myself together. This was definitely the bull ride of all bull rides. We were all trying to hold on for dear life. Seven family members were weeping and crying out. God showed up big time.

Job Gets Chastised. Joshua Faces the Walls of Jericho. Samson Brings Down the House. What a wonder of wonders Jehovah is! To think He can take ordinary men and women and give them strength to overcome their enemy, to scale any mountain before them.

And then, with the same superpowers, God showed up for us. The discernible presence of the Holy Spirit was unmistakeably in that tiny cabin aboard ship where our precious Candace had gone to be with the Lord.

We lifted our hands toward heaven and started to thank the Lord for her life. We sang. We quoted God's Word. We truly praised the God who meets us in the midst of life's storms. We were still in pain, but the Lord was ministering to our souls.

And Jeromy, who has loved and walked with God since the day he was born, raised his hands and—of all things—began to laugh. Though they were two very different people, Candace and Jeromy couldn't have loved each other more. The God of All Comfort did an amazing thing for our son. Jeromy continued to laugh and praise God. Then with a voice similar to a lion's roar, he declared, "I can see her. I can see her. She's riding a horse. She's not sick. She's happy and laughing and riding in heaven." Not only was our son comforted, but God ministered to all our hearts.

We were just working men and women. We were—and still are—ordinary people striving to live in a way that would honor our Heavenly Father. We still get up every day and deal with issues one at a time. When Candace died, He reached out and took us by the hand.

The Lord assured me, "Don't worry. Where Candace and I are, you will also come one day. Meanwhile, Roger, do me a favor. Keep working. Work hard at your job. Work extra hard raising your family and loving your wife. Give it all you can to be a friend to a stranger and help those in need. Never be lazy. Don't set your mind on material things but on those things that last for all eternity. And remember this: I am with you always—even unto the end. Don't doubt it for a minute. I, the Lord your God, love a working man."

And He'll be there for you too. Will everything be easy? No way. Will all your problems disappear? No. But will the God of the Working Man see you through and give you all the power you need? You bet He will. He'll stick with you, closer than a brother. God will never leave you alone.

The Ultimate Superhero can heal a broken marriage. He can multiply that last hundred dollars in a bank account. He can restore a broken body—or give the strength to persevere through the affliction.

God mends fractured families. He hears our prayers and ministers to our friends and family. He sets free those who alone can't overcome the bonds of addiction to drugs, alcohol, and sex. The Lord sees the repentant murderer in his prison cell, and by His grace, pours out peace. No roof over our head? No food in our stomach? No money in the bank? God is there to reach out His mighty hand and free us from Satan's clutches. He also delivers us from lust, pride, and countless other sins that lead us down the road to eternal death.

And what can we do? Admit our screw ups, our sins. Ask God to forgive us. Accept Christ as our Savior and walk with Him from here on, getting to know Him better by reading His Word and hanging out with His other kids. Remember, Jesus is the real Superhero and, without a doubt, He loves the working man.

Heart of a Sold Out Believer

(Author Unknown)

Today I'm stepping across the line. I'm tired of waiting. I'm finished with wavering. I made my choice. The verdict is in. My decision is binding. There is no turning back!

I will live the rest of my life serving God's purposes with God's people according to God's plan for God's glory. I will use my life to celebrate His presence, cultivate His character, demonstrate His love, and communicate His message. Since my past has been forgiven, I refuse to waste any more time on shallow living, petty thinking, thoughtless doing, useless regretting, hurtful resenting, or faithless worrying.

Instead, I will magnify the Lord, grow to maturity, serve in ministry, and fulfill my mission in the membership of His family.

Because this life is preparation for the next, I will value worship over wealth; we over me; character over comfort; service over status; and people over possessions, positions, and pleasures. I know what matters most and I will give it all I have. I will do the best I can with what I have for Jesus today. I will not be captivated by culture, manipulated by critics, motivated by praise, frustrated by problems, turned away by temptation, or intimidated by the devil.

I will just keep running with my eyes on the prize. Not focused on fear or overwhelmed by bad news, when times get tough and I get tired, I will not back up, back off, back down, back out, or backslide. I will just keep moving forward by God's grace. I am Spirit-led, spiritually-driven, and mission-minded.

I cannot be bought. I will not be compromised. I shall not quit until I finish my race!

I am a trophy of God's amazing grace so I will be gracious to everyone, grateful for each and every day, and I will be generous with everything God entrusts to me. To my Lord and Savior Jesus Christ, the One who took my place on the cross, I say, "However, whenever, and whatever You ask me to do, I will do it. My answer, in advance, is yes. Wherever You lead and no matter the cost, I am ready. Anytime, anyway, anyplace . . . whatever it takes, Lord. Whatever it takes!"

This is the heart of a sold out believer!

Consider this . . .

1. *If you are a Christian* . . . Are you sold out to Jesus? It's time. God has a great big plan for your life and He is standing by to help you live the plan. Are you willing? Do you want to make a difference—an eternal difference? You can. Focus on Jesus. Pray. Study God's Word. Have you been helped by the thoughts in this book? Consider getting a group of your buddies together to read the book and meet once a week . . . or once a month . . . to talk about what you are learning. To share the ups and downs you are experiencing. To encourage once another and pray for one another. Help each other develop the heart of a sold out believer!

2. *If you are not a Christian* . . . As I've shared in this book, I have done some pretty serious bull riding. I've traveled some rugged terrain. Let me tell you, I'd never have made it

without Jesus. I know He loves me no matter what. I know He is with me no matter what. I know He has forgiven my sins. I know when my life on this earth is finished, I will be in heaven with Him forever. And with Candace and all those I care about who belong to Him and went before me.

How about you? Do you want those things for yourself? You can have them. Right now.

You see, God is a holy God. No sin can enter his presence. And that's a problem because we have all sinned. Every one of us. But, incredibly, God loves us and wants us to be with Him forever. So He made a way. Jesus, His Son, came to earth and lived here about 33 years. He taught. He loved. He healed. He was criticized. He was lied about. He was betrayed. And finally He was crucified. Why? Because He loves us.

Jesus lived a perfect life here on earth. He shed his blood on the cross to pay the penalty for our sin. And then He rose from death the third day to live forever.

So how can this make a difference in your life? He made it so simple. Just believe. Believe you have sinned. Believe Jesus is the Son of God. Believe he paid the penalty by dying on the cross. Believe He arose.

> If you confess with your mouth that Jesus is Lord and believe in your heart that God raised him from the dead, you will be saved. For it is by believing in your heart that you are made right with God, and it is by confessing with your mouth that you are saved. As the Scriptures tell us, "Anyone who trusts in him will never be disgraced." Jew and Gentile are the same in this respect. They have the same Lord,

who gives generously to all who call on him. For "Everyone who calls on the name of the LORD will be saved."(Romans 10:9-13 NLT)

Are you ready? Just talk to God. Tell Him you believe. Tell Him you want to follow Jesus Christ.

Have you taken this step? Let me be the first to welcome you to the family of God. Want to talk? Send me an email at georgerogerlee@gmail.com. I'd love to hear from you.

You'll still have some bull riding to do, some obstacles to move. But now you have a Friend who loves you unconditionally and will be with you through it all. Don't try to do it alone. He offers His strength, His power. Jesus is truly the Real Superhero.